How to Find Joy in a Capitalist Hellscape

How to Find Joy in a Capitalist Hellscape

Elsie Gilmore

HOW TO FIND JOY IN A CAPITALIST HELLSCAPE. Copyright © 2024 by Elsie Gilmore. All rights reserved. No part of this book may be used or reproduced in any manner whatsoever without written permission except in the case of brief quotations embodied in critical articles and reviews.

First Edition: October 2024

Paperback ISBN: 979-8-9908728-0-6

Ebook ISBN: 979-8-9908728-1-3

Cover and interior illustrations by Yanuary Navarro at yanuary.com

Author illustration by Letisia Cruz at lesinfin.com

This book is dedicated to all those who choose to stay kind in an often unkind world.

And also to my 10-year-old self, who didn't think any of this was possible.

Contents

INTRODUCTION
    WHAT IS CAPITALISM?   3
    POPE FRANCIS ON CAPITALISM   9
    WHAT IS JOY?   11
    ONE LAST THING... OK TWO   13

MIND
    INTRO   17
    LEARN TO BE PRESENT   19
    MASTER YOUR EMOTIONS   23
    FOCUS ON WHAT'S IMPORTANT   26
    PRACTICE GRATITUDE   28
    LOOK WITHIN FOR JOY AND HAPPINESS   30
    KNOW THAT WE'RE NOT OUR THOUGHTS   32

CULTIVATE EMPATHY	34
TREAT YOURSELF LIKE SOMEONE YOU LOVE	37
TAKE CARE OF YOUR MENTAL HEALTH	39
RESOURCES	41

BODY

INTRO	45
FUEL YOUR BODY RIGHT	47
MOVE IT OR LOSE IT	50
PRACTICE HEALING AND RESTING	53
AVOID EXCESS	55
GET COMFORTABLE WITH YOUR SEXUALITY	57
LEARN WHAT YOUR BODY IS CAPABLE OF	59
FIGHT FOR BODILY AUTONOMY	60
RESOURCES	63

RELATIONSHIPS

INTRO	67
SURROUND YOURSELF WITH GOOD PEOPLE	69

MAKE AUTHENTIC CONNECTIONS	71
LEARN TO COMMUNICATE	73
DON'T BE SO JUDGY	77
DON'T STEREOTYPE GROUPS	80
SEE THE GOOD IN PEOPLE	85
SET HEALTHY BOUNDARIES	87
NOT EVERYONE WILL LIKE YOU AND THAT'S OK	90
LEARN TO ENJOY YOUR OWN COMPANY	92
TALK TO STRANGERS	94
RESOURCES	96

WORK

INTRO	99
WORK TO LIVE. DON'T LIVE TO WORK.	101
AVOID HUSTLE CULTURE	103
BUILD TANGIBLE SKILLS	106
CREATE YOUR OWN PATH AND OPPORTUNITIES	108
MAKE YOUR OWN DEFINITION OF SUCCESS	110

- FOCUS ON THE DIRECTION YOU WANT TO GO ... 113
- FIGHT THE URGE TO COMPETE ... 116
- MAKE YOUR BUSINESS CAPITAL-ISM-PROOF ... 118
- DON'T COMPARE YOURSELF TO WHERE OTHERS ARE ... 119
- OWN LESS STUFF TO WORK LESS ... 121
- RESOURCES ... 123

MONEY
- INTRO ... 127
- KNOW YOUR MONEY PRIORITIES ... 129
- IMPLEMENT A "NO BUY" JANUARY ... 132
- DON'T BE IN A HURRY ... 134
- SEE THINGS AS THEY ARE ... 136
- DITCH FOMO TO SAVE MONEY ... 138
- VOTE WITH YOUR DOLLARS ... 140
- SEE THINGS AS INVESTMENTS AND TOOLS ... 142
- DON'T FALL FOR SUBSCRIPTIONS ... 144
- BELIEVE IN ABUNDANCE ... 145

RESOURCES	147
CREATIVITY	
INTRO	151
BE CREATIVE JUST BECAUSE	152
DON'T BE AFRAID TO SUCK AT SOMETHING NEW	154
MAKE EVERY DAY AN ADVENTURE	156
FIND CREATIVE ALTERNATIVES TO "NEW"	158
EXPLORE ACTIVITIES THAT DON'T COST MONEY	160
FILL YOUR LIFE WITH BEAUTY AND COMFORT	162
EMBRACE THE EXPERIENCE OF LIFE	164
RESOURCES	165
COMMUNITY	
INTRO	169
FIND YOUR PEOPLE	171
KNOW THAT WE ARE INTERDEPENDENT	173
GIVE BACK LOCALLY	175

ASK FOR HELP	177
PARTICIPATE IN YOUR COMMUNITY	178
HUG EVERYONE	179
BE A CHEERLEADER	182
PLANT SOMETHING	184
TREAD LIGHTLY	186
RESOURCES	188

SPIRITUALITY

INTRO	191
WISH FOR THE BEST FOR YOURSELF AND OTHERS	192
PRIORITIZE JOY	195
BELIEVE IN SOMETHING	198
SPEND TIME IN NATURE	201
HAVE RITUALS	203
RADIATE PEACE	204
GIVE PEOPLE GRACE	205
RESOURCES	207

CIVICS

INTRO	211
BE KIND	212

GIVE A SHIT ABOUT SOMETHING	216
EXERCISE YOUR DUTY TO VOTE	218
JOIN A MOVEMENT	220
LEARN ABOUT COLONIALISM AND PATRIARCHY	222
RAGE AGAINST THE MACHINE	226
BUT DON'T FALL FOR OUTRAGE BAIT	228
DON'T GET DISTRACTED	230
PARTICIPATE	232
TRAVEL	234
BE A PEACEMAKER	235
RESOURCES	237

THE STUFF AT THE END

CONCLUSION	241
MANIFESTO OF JOY	243
SHOUT-OUTS	244
CITATIONS	245

INTRODUCTION

WHAT IS CAPITALISM?

> *"And because many of us live under capitalism, in cultures committed to the belief that material possessions can heal spiritual wounds, we have been convinced that economic dominance can fill up our cup of value and worth. And yet misery, suffering, rage, and despair abound."*[1]
>
> adrienne maree brown

A joy-filled life is something anyone can attain, and it's something everyone deserves. This book is about discovering ways to live with more joy under capitalism. So, first, let's talk about what capitalism is (and isn't).

Capitalism is a system of extracting wealth from people's labor and the Earth's resources and turning that into immense profit for a small number of people. Over time, the capitalist owner class in the United States and elsewhere has paid themselves more and their employees less to create an enormous wealth gap between the super-rich and everyone else. This inequality is a feature of capitalism, not a bug.

When I refer to capitalism in this book, I am not referring to small, independent businesses in your neighborhood or online. I'm not referring to farmers markets or artisans. I'm definitely not referring to the young ladies selling Girl Scout cookies in front of your local grocery store (although they can be aggressive).

When I use the term capitalism or capitalist, I'm referring to large corporations and the economic system that depends on worker exploitation, environmental degradation, profit maximization at all costs, disposable goods, shrinkflation, aggressive marketing, manipulative sales tactics, and all the forces working together to try to get you to spend your hard-earned money on things you don't want or need for the benefit of a few and at the expense of many. Capitalism also captures things you need that they know you can't avoid buying, like groceries, housing, and medical care... things people should not be making enormous profits from.

What else makes big corporations so bad, you might ask? First, most of them do not value the people who make their company run. Companies often funnel more profits to their owners and investors instead of raising worker wages. They see employees as commodities instead of the real live human beings without whom their businesses wouldn't run. Secondly, corporations can sometimes get away with unsafe or unhealthy working conditions, especially if they've used what could've been your extra wages to bank some profit, which they can then use to pay fines for failed health inspections. These are just a few examples of the unsavory things corporations do.

Many companies are engaged in the extraction of natural resources (trees, water, minerals, soil, and other plants and animals), which can be devastating to the health of surrounding communities. Mining raw materials is often done in countries with little protection for the people there. Sometimes, there is bloody conflict surrounding the ownership of these resources. Some companies, like Walmart, create competitive conditions that undercut the profits of their suppliers, some of whom are small businesses that don't have much leverage to fight back. On top of all that, corporations often hide their profits in other countries so they don't have to pay taxes that could help improve the lives of other Americans.

While I was getting my Master's in Environmental Law & Policy from Vermont Law School (shout out to my alma mater), I learned for the first time about the asbestos industry. In the mid-1800s, asbestos was becoming popular in many home construction products because of its fire resistance. These items included concrete, bricks, ceiling insulation, roofing, and flooring. In the late 1800's, it began to emerge that people working around this stuff were getting ill with lung diseases, including cancer. Because the companies making and selling it didn't want to lose any profit, their solution was to deny, deny, deny, and continue to expand sales of asbestos. But eventually, they couldn't cover it up because they were getting sued. So, they came up with what they determined to be the value of a human life and used it to calculate whether they could still be profitable if a few people died (and they had to pay out settlements). That's right. They used the death of someone's father or daughter or cousin to help predict their future profitability.

And that, my friends, is when I knew big corporations were a large part of what's wrong with the world.

(Incidentally, asbestos still kills at least 3,000 Americans a year.[2] It was outlawed in the US in 1989 but then reinstated in 1991 when the chemical industry successfully sued to overturn that ruling. Do you see the problem? It remained legal until this year when it was again banned.)[3]

While it seems that we average people are at the mercy of capitalism, the system could not exist without our labor and our spending. That means we power capitalism on both ends. That is why workers strike - because they know the business can't run without them. Products aren't produced. Services aren't rendered. Without us. If we decided to, we could bring capitalism to its knees - first by not working and secondly by not spending.

Along with striking and boycotting, one of the best ways to fight back against capitalism is to find joy. Seems silly, right? But capitalism does not want us to be happy. In fact, it depends on us being unhappy so that it can sell us its products and propaganda.

It wants us to be unhappy and apathetic so we won't fight back against the injustice it causes. Furthermore, it wants you to blame the problems of the world on others and not them.

But we don't have to let capitalism (powerful people, Wall Street, big business) sell us hopelessness, loneliness, fatalism, or their products.

Maybe, like me, you didn't grow up with joy. Maybe you only knew how to look at the world through a negative lens. Perhaps no one taught you how to feel joy and see the world as the amazing place that it is, full of beauty, wonder, and wonderful people.

As a rejection of capitalism, I did not live a very conventional life, nor did I do all the things capitalism wanted me to do. In fact, when I was young, I looked around and saw how unhappy many of those around me were. They all had the idea that you should sacrifice your whole life to make a profit for someone else and only then get to enjoy the fruits of your labor in retirement.

I rejected that notion, especially as labor unions waned and companies stopped offering the generous retirement benefits of the past. Plus, many people never even live to see retirement.

As a creative person, many of the jobs available to me, especially in my rural hometown, felt stifling. I wasn't cut out for working in an office on administrative tasks, which is what many women in my town were relegated to. There was no joy in that for me, so I ended up starting my own business. As someone who is not a capitalist, that worked only because what I was doing (web development) was pioneering. I was very good at it and gained all my business from referrals, so I didn't have to do any hard selling.

I'm also an activist, so it's imperative that I find joy in life to keep me from feeling hopeless about the world. (Activism can be very draining because we focus on the problems that need fixing.) This act of resistance keeps me fighting for the places, people, and things that make the world beautiful.

There is much joy to be found despite capitalism's attempt to control all aspects of our lives, and I hope this guide will help you find it. This book is not about how to live entirely outside the capitalist system. It's about how to survive, thrive, and be alive inside it while we work to dismantle the worst parts of it. With this book as inspiration, you can use your limitless imagination to find more ways to avoid feeding the capitalist machine. Flip to any section of this book to find practical ways to find joy, resist capitalism, and make the world a better place.

POPE FRANCIS ON CAPITALISM

In Pope Francis's 2015 encyclical called "On Care For Our Common Home,"[4] he called for a new way of doing things, saying this (summarized) about capitalism:

1. Technology and Profit Over People: Our focus on technology and making money harms both the environment and society. This mindset prioritizes profit and power over what's good for people.

2. Markets Aren't Fixing Things: Hoping market growth will solve our problems is unrealistic. Markets often ignore the needs of the poor and the environment, leading to more exploitation and damage.

3. Growing Inequality: Capitalism, as it stands, creates a lot of inequality and exploitation. The constant push for more profit helps a small number of people while making life harder for the majority, especially the poor and marginalized.

4. Consumerism and Waste: Our consumer culture, where we buy and throw away a lot, is unsustainable. It leads to too much waste and environmental harm, ignoring the fact that the Earth's resources are limited.

5. Need for Ethical Responsibility: We should change how we do things to focus on ethical responsibility and the common good. This means promoting sustainable practices, protecting the environment, and ensuring justice for everyone, especially the vulnerable and future generations.

So saith the leader of the Catholic world. Fuck yeah.

WHAT IS JOY?

Joy is a feeling of fullness, kind of like a food coma. In fact, a food coma – that feeling of ecstatic fullness from gorging on yummy foods – is a form of joy.

Joy is something we can experience by hiking up a mountain or by staring silently at a perfectly still lake. Joy is when we watch a bird land on a nearby tree and listen to his song. It's dancing in the rain or enjoying a meal with a group of people you love.

Joy is an awareness of something special about the world or about an object, person, animal, or landscape. It is a feeling of closeness to people, beings, or nature. It is a feeling of belonging. A feeling of contentedness.

Joy is a feeling that we can transfer from one person to another through our words and actions.

Joy is also something that needs to be recharged. It's a practice. We need to keep cultivating and experiencing joy so we will stay optimistic about the world. Experiencing joy motivates us to keep fighting for the planet and for each other.

In short, joy is all around us, and we need it to get through life without being miserable. We can find it alone or with others, but we need to keep prioritizing it in order for its impact on us to last.

ONE LAST THING... OK TWO

First: I've included the names of kickass books you should read. Please buy them either at a locally owned bookstore near you or on Bookshop.org instead of that other large, exploitative online retailer. You can even select your local bookstore to benefit from the purchase on Bookshop.org.

Second: You will not agree with everything I've written here, perhaps especially the part about being kind to people you don't like, but believe me when I say that the way forward is for all of us to find common ground and work together.

Final note: I am not a psychiatrist, doctor, money expert, or lawyer, so please follow my advice only after doing your own due diligence. My favorite local yoga instructor reminds us throughout class that if our bodies cannot do the poses as originally designed, we should make modifications that fit our bodies and comfort levels. Any way of doing a pose is the right way if it works for you. That's the advice I will give you for reading this book. It's OK to modify anything I say so that it works for you, as long as it's done with the original spirit.

MIND

INTRO

Keeping our minds healthy is one of our most important jobs. Without a healthy mind, we will be less likely to have healthy relationships and a peaceful life. Without healthy relationships, it will be difficult to find joy as we struggle to survive in this capitalist hellscape.

Growing up, my family members weren't great at communicating. They tended to hold resentments inside without expressing them and then explode with emotions once they could no longer stay quiet. They also tended to be defensive, so communicating with them was often like tiptoeing around landmines.

Because of this, I spent a lot of time processing things in my head. I played back scenarios from the past over and over again and worried about future interactions that would undoubtedly leave me feeling misunderstood and hurt. All of this overthinking tore me away from my enjoyment of life.

Consequently, I did not enter adulthood with strong emotional intelligence, leaving me not knowing how to have healthy relationships (or find joy). I carried the bad habits I'd learned in childhood with me through a rocky second decade of life until I learned a better way. The following are things I had to learn, through trial and lots of error, in order to find joy later in life.

LEARN TO BE PRESENT

Being present is truly the best way to fill your life with joy.

When we are in our head instead of present in the moment, we don't notice the details around us - the people, nature, music, and things that could bring us joy as we go along our journey if we only pay attention. Joy is in the details of life.

The worries of capitalism can cause our minds to run at 1000 miles a minute. We have bills to pay. Our job is demanding. Our rent is going up. One of our friends is struggling financially. We are straight-up exhausted.

Being present is something you can do for free that capitalism can't take away from you. We get to choose how to use our minds every day.

We can choose to sit down with friends and not look at our phones. We can choose to show up for life without being distracted. We can choose to make space to not worry, space that is just about savoring life. That doesn't mean we shouldn't take care of the important things that are causing us stress. It just means that carrying those things around with us every moment will only compound the negative impacts on our bodies and minds.

To enjoy life, we can learn to immerse ourselves in it. We can savor the food we eat. We can pay attention to the sounds we hear in nature. We can delight in the sight of a bird or a painted mural.

We can get better at this by practicing mindfulness or, as I like to also call it, "noticing."

Noticing is something you can practice for only 10 minutes a day with tremendous benefits. Then, you can take that "practice" and apply it to other aspects of your life.

Noticing is about learning to be present. It's about training your mind to give less importance to all the thoughts floating around in it so you can be attentive to what's actually happening around you.

If you want to practice noticing, try this 5-10 minute exercise:

Step 1: Find a comfy spot to sit

You can do this practice on the couch, your office chair, at the dining room table, or any place you are safe and comfortable. Turn off excess noise, such as the radio or television. Sit in a posture that is upright so your body is not crumpled over. You can place your hands in your lap or anywhere you like.

Step 2: Ground yourself in the moment

I recommend closing your eyes for this exercise. Those of us with acutely tuned-in senses have enough data pouring in. Let's close off one of those portals so we can focus better.

Take five slow, deep breaths. Concentrate on the action of filling your lungs with air and emptying them in one long exhale. Drop your shoulders on each exhale. Let your body relax.

Notice what is going on in the physical world around you. Can you hear birds? Is there traffic noise? Is your air conditioning running? Is it warm? Cold? Are there any smells? How does your bum feel on this seat? Immerse yourself in the senses of this moment. Focus on what you can feel, hear, and smell. If another thought pops up, notice it and return to your senses.

Step 3: Take inventory of what is inside you

What's going on inside your body? Are you hungry? Do you have any aches and pains? Are you tired? Do you feel energized? Notice all your physical sensations, but don't veer off into other thoughts about them.

What's going on inside your mind? Are you feeling sad? Do you feel happy? Are you stressed or anxious? Do not go into a long narrative about why any of these feelings exist. Simply notice and note them. Don't make judgments about anything you notice. This is a time to notice and move on. You're taking inventory, not writing a novel. Simply notice your different emotional and mental states without commentary.

> *"Acknowledge the feeling, give it your full, compassionate, even welcoming attention, and even if it's only for a few seconds, drop the story line about the feeling.*

> *This allows you to have a direct experience of it, free of interpretation. Don't fuel it with concepts or opinions about whether it's good or bad. Just be present with the sensation."*[5]
>
> Pema Chodron

When you are done noticing all your physical and mental/emotional states, sit quietly for a few minutes, acknowledging that you are safe and present in that moment. Often, our anxiety creates problems that don't exist, but we can acknowledge that there is no emergency in this moment, even if there are issues that need addressing.

As you go through your day, try to remember this feeling of being present. Stay grounded in the physical sensations of living while you eat, work, and play. You may be surprised at the clarity and focus you gain that will help you make better decisions.

MASTER YOUR EMOTIONS

"If we become aware of what's happening before we act, behaviour becomes a function of choice rather than a result of an impulse or trigger. You begin to control your world more as opposed to the outside world controlling you."[6]

Marshall Goldsmith

Some people go through life with little idea of how to control their emotions and subsequently end up on a constant rollercoaster of emotional states. In relationships, this might look like frequent drama and fights.

When we find we are overreacting to things a partner or friend says or does, we may be experiencing a trigger. A trigger is an emotional response that may be related to an event in our memory. For instance, if your romantic partner raises their voice during an argument, it might unconsciously remind you of when your parents frequently yelled at each other. You may react to your partner in a way that is disproportionate to what they've done because you are feeling a strong emotion from your past.

It is more than OK to experience these emotions, but we should take responsibility for how we act them out. We don't want to blow up at people for things that happened in our past. We can learn the difference between what happened then and what is happening now.

We can start by asking ourselves why we reacted the way we did. Was it really about what our partner said or did? If not, what were we reminded of? Something one of our parents did? Or a former partner?

Please note: this is not an invitation to tolerate bad behavior from people. This is an invitation to examine where our emotional reactions are coming from and deal with them appropriately. Sometimes, we act out because of stress, work pressure, or other issues we're dealing with. Capitalism's stranglehold on your life may have you hovering at the raw edge of your nervous system.

No matter the cause of our raw emotions, we can hold ourselves accountable for our emotional responses. Do we need to talk to a therapist about it? Can we learn to recognize when we are having an emotional reaction? Can we talk to our partner, friend, or family member about ways they could help reduce the impact of our triggers?

Becoming more aware and being able to pull out of those automatic emotional responses in the moment is a valuable skill.

Dramatic emotional outbursts can cause stress for those around you if it seems like you're frequently being unreasonable.

We can also become triggered by posts or comments on social media that are mean or outrageous. These posts/comments were often made specifically to get a rise out of us emotionally. When someone can easily control our emotions, they have power over us. We don't need to be quick to respond to every comment we find offensive or objectionable. Take a breath. Scroll on by. Let it go. You've got better things to do than let internet trolls waste your time. You can learn to know when to say nothing and when to make a thoughtful, measured response to something you disagree with.

Having control of your emotions can improve your relationships and bring you more peace and stability. It can contribute to a sense of joy in your life that makes you more immune to the enticing draw of capitalism.

This is all part of mastering our emotions.

FOCUS ON WHAT'S IMPORTANT

Our attention has become a valuable commodity to social media companies and advertisers. They want our eyeballs on their ads for the maximum amount of time every day, and they would prefer we don't pursue joy-seeking activities in favor of doom-scrolling or looking at cat videos (that are interspersed with ads). Social media companies created their product to maximize the dopamine hits that our minds crave.

But our attention is something we can control, and we need it to focus on our work, family, health, hobbies, etc. If we spend too much of it mindlessly scrolling social media, that is taking away from other beneficial activities (or rest) we could be engaging in. We're also exposing ourselves to the tidal wave of ads that capitalism wants to serve us.

When we choose to focus our attention on things that bring us joy (like a walk in nature, time with family, or pursuing our favorite hobby), we honor ourselves and our health. When we spend less time scrolling through our social media feeds, we take away the power advertisers have to compel us to buy things.

While scrolling online often results in me learning new things (which I enjoy), it can become a distraction from the focus I'd like to have on the most important things in my life. Going down the rabbit hole occasionally is OK, but it can cost me time that could've been spent more constructively or joyfully.

A consistently fragmented attention span makes it harder for us to focus when we really need to. The constant dopamine hits from checking social media cause our minds to search for those hits even when we're trying to complete a longer task (like writing a book) or engage in person with friends or loved ones.

We can train our minds to be more focused by creating good habits. There are ways we can limit our social media time that include setting timers, only using it during lunch or at night, or using an app on our phone that disables it during certain hours. This opens up our time for creative endeavors and for time with other humans in person.

While shifting our focus habits isn't easy, it can make a profound difference in our lives. We have the power to choose what we pay attention to.

PRACTICE GRATITUDE

"Abundance is connected with a deep sense of gratitude."[7]

Jack Kornfield

Gratitude comes from a deep place within us, and it happens when we stop taking things for granted or mindlessly consuming life.

Gratitude sometimes requires us to experience comparison feelings like lack, fear, or pain... to make us appreciate the little, meaningful things in life. Many times, I am grateful not to have a migraine – to just enjoy a day without pain.

Capitalism does not want us to feel gratitude because gratitude often means we are content with what we have and where we are. It's the opposite of striving for more. Capitalism wants us to stay hungry for the next purchase. If we take time to be grateful, we have slowed down. And when we slow down, we have time to think. And when we have time to think, we realize how ugly the rat race for the American dream is. As a result, we may strive less, appreciate what we have, and know that it is enough.

Gratitude is something we should express to others who help bring joy to our lives or who simply do any kind thing for us, no matter how small. Tell people you appreciate them and how they've made your life better. Thank the cashier, the mailman, your coworker, your partner, and all the people who add to your day. You can't imagine how unappreciated some of those folks probably feel. You can add a ray of sunshine to their day by genuinely thanking them for their contribution to the world and to your day. You can even feel grateful toward people who weren't so nice to you because they may have helped you learn a valuable lesson. (But you don't have to tell them that.)

When you wake up in the morning and before you go to bed are great times to think about all the things you're grateful for. Take a deep breath and let gratitude fill your body.

LOOK WITHIN FOR JOY AND HAPPINESS

When I was in my 20s, I realized that not only was I not happy but that it probably wasn't normal to be so unhappy - especially in your 20s. Many of the people around me were also unhappy, and I didn't think that was normal either.

I spent much of my 20s looking for happiness "out there" in alcohol or relationships or purchases or trips. Those things provided temporary feelings of happiness (and often provided great memories), but when they were gone, the unhappiness returned (and my wallet was often drained).

In my 30s, I finally began to see that happiness was not "out there." Happiness was something I could choose. Being single for most of my 30s made me realize, first and foremost, that there was more to life than looking for a partner. I could just be single and be content. I could work on my career, take trips, spend time with friends, and do anything I wanted. I could just be content right then and not feel like happiness was something that happened in the future when I had a certain someone, owned certain possessions, or had accomplished certain things. I didn't have to put off happiness.

Something I also learned is that happiness is not a constant state. No one is happy 100% of the time. That's not normal. We all have fluctuating emotions. In my life, I try to focus on being content and accepting all that life throws at me with grace – good or bad. Contentment brings peace and calm through uncertain times. It is about cultivating a feeling of acceptance in each moment.

Joy, contentment, and happiness are within us all the time. We simply have to decide to prioritize them over grasping for the future or looking for solutions "out there."

KNOW THAT WE'RE NOT OUR THOUGHTS

In an average day, our mind is filled with all kinds of thoughts. Some are neutral, but others are sad, angry, frustrated, or confused.

Any thought or feeling you have is valid, but it's important to know that the thought or feeling isn't you. You are simply experiencing the thought or feeling.

A good way to change your language about thoughts and feelings is to say that you are "feeling sad" instead of you "are sad." You, the person, are not a sad person. You are a person having sad feelings. By looking at it this way, we do not define ourselves by our thoughts and feelings, which are often fleeting.

You are a person having experiences, thoughts, and feelings. But none of them describe your whole person. Everyone, including you, has likes and dislikes, hopes and dreams, and habits, both good and bad. Take the time to use language that does not diminish yourself or others, even people you don't like.

It's easy to see people you don't like as defined by a single characteristic, but that is never true. It may be an easy way for you to look at things, but it obscures the complex nature of people and denies them their full humanity.

It's good to examine and challenge your thoughts so you don't pigeonhole yourself or others.

CULTIVATE EMPATHY

The anonymity of social media makes it easy to forget about the humanity of someone whose comment you're responding to. The news has become entertainment and is often incredibly sensationalized, further removing us from the reality being shown. It might be easy to watch the news sometimes and think you're watching a movie instead of actual people suffering and dying.

You may become detached from your emotions about these scenes either because they don't seem relevant to you or because you have emotional overload and just can't keep up the level of anger, fear, or sadness that would be normal when seeing the things shown (war, environmental degradation, natural disasters, terrible accidents).

Many of the folks in charge of the capitalist train wreck want you to see people who are different than you as "others." What they don't tell you is that each of those "others" has a story, and most of those "others" are good people, just like you. Capitalism purposely doesn't want you to humanize them because often capitalism is dropping bombs on them or failing to provide them with adequate social services.

Many people are unhappy about capitalism but have been told the problems in their lives lie elsewhere... with "those people." (For instance: people of color, Republicans, Democrats, immigrants, poor people, working-class people, union members, teachers, furries, drag queens or protesters.) Capitalism is always trying to deflect blame away from itself by finding a scapegoat.

Think about the people or groups of people you don't like. Why don't you like them? Think about why they might act the way they act. Have they been marginalized? Have corporations harmed them? (Like closing factories and moving them to China.) Have they, like you, been the victims of the infamous and impotent "trickle-down economics?"

How might their relationship with capitalism make them act poorly? How might the people they look up to be misleading them? How do you think this makes them feel? Maybe they feel misunderstood and powerless. Maybe they're afraid and frustrated. Maybe you are, too.

Trying to understand how other people feel and what their experiences have been is the foundation for empathy. It's easy to look at someone's behavior and call them a bad person. But most things people do have motivations and reasons. These reasons are not a justification or excuse for bad behavior, but this exercise can help us to put ourselves in others' shoes. Not everyone is alike in how they deal with feelings of frustration and betrayal. Not everyone has supportive and loving people around them or the resources to make their life less challenging.

In Purposeful Empathy, author Anita Nowak says, "If we care about humanity and life in our planet, we must seek alternative economic approaches animated by a new set of values, including empathy."[8]

Capitalism has no empathy, but we can.

TREAT YOURSELF LIKE SOMEONE YOU LOVE

Sometimes, we are raised to put ourselves last by parents who think our sole purpose in life should be to serve others (especially if we are women). There may be good intentions behind this, but many times, the implementation means that we give more of ourselves than we should and are not left with sufficient time, energy, or resources for ourselves.

We often don't treat ourselves the way we would treat a friend. We talk harshly to ourselves, never giving ourselves a break if we make a mistake. We work too hard without enough rest.

But there's no joy in putting yourself last. We can speak to ourselves with love. We can lift ourselves up. We can be our own cheerleaders. We can leave encouraging messages around our home, such as: "You can do it!" "I believe in you!" "You're capable!"

So, here's my advice:
- Treat your body with kindness. Feed it healthy, nutritious food. Drink lots of water. Take regular walks.

- Treat your mind with kindness. Meditate. Don't focus on bad news or dark thoughts.

- Saving money is good, but don't forget to invest in yourself. Take a class to learn something new or fun. Take yourself on a fun adventure.

Don't be fooled, though. Capitalism will try to make you feel insecure and maybe like you aren't good enough. It might make you think that you "deserve" things that aren't good for you, either because they're too expensive or because they will physically make you less healthy. No one "deserves" a night out with alcohol. A night out with alcohol is OK sometimes, but alcohol is inherently bad for you. So, it's not a treat because you love yourself. It's a treat because you want to indulge in something.

Capitalism might try to convince you that you want a new car that you don't need, but putting yourself in debt is not loving yourself. Thinking about whether it would be best for your future and goals is loving yourself. Sometimes loving yourself is indulging, and sometimes it's being practical. Sometimes, you really do need a car, and that's OK. (But don't buy new off the lot because that's just a waste of money.)

As long as you're mindful about it, you will make good decisions for yourself that are based on caring for yourself and not based on impulsiveness caused by the marketing strategies employed by capitalism.

TAKE CARE OF YOUR MENTAL HEALTH

Our mental health can greatly affect our physical health. Stress caused by unhealthy work environments, financial strain, and the negative atmosphere that capitalism perpetuates can manifest as pain in our bodies. Some people also have mental health issues not related to capitalism, and that can't be solved solely with mindfulness practices.

Not everyone is fortunate enough to have easy access to affordable mental health care, but if you do, don't be afraid to use it. Not only should mental healthcare be free in the U.S., it should be mandatory! Everyone can benefit from it and should not feel ashamed or weird about using it.

If you don't have insurance, you can try one of the low-cost app-based or online mental health services. Something is better than nothing, and talking to a neutral party can help you sort out your issues in ways telling a close friend may not. A professional can also assess any additional treatments that might benefit you, including prescription medications if they are warranted.

You deserve mental health care and should include it as part of your pursuit of joy. Taking care of your body, as outlined in the next chapter, also goes a long way toward a healthy mind.

RESOURCES

BOOKS:

How to Do Nothing by Jenny Odell
You Are Not What You Think by David Richo
The Mastery of Self by Don Miguel Ruiz Jr
The Missing Piece by Shel Silverstein
Triggers by David Richo

HOMEWORK:

Try to make it a habit to start your day off with 10 minutes of noticing practice.

Every evening, write down three things about your day for which you feel grateful. Looking back over these items in the future can remind you of the good in your life.

BODY

INTRO

There are few things more important than keeping our body healthy. This is one of our main responsibilities to ourselves, those we love, and to society as a whole.

It is much more difficult to live a life of joy when our body is broken or ill because we have neglected it. Everyone will get sick or hurt sometimes, but there are many ways people get sick that are a direct result of the way they treat their bodies.

If you live in the U.S., like me, you also know that it can be expensive to get sick. To be honest, part of the reason I keep myself healthy is to avoid the costs of doctors, hospitals, and prescriptions. It's cheaper for me to take walks and eat veggies.

The pharmaceutical industry is a scourge of hungry capitalists. They want to sell you all their pills, many of which are made to relieve the symptoms of their other pills. Before you know it, you're taking five pills for one ailment because the first pill had so many side effects.

If you have good insurance, it might feel "easy" to take prescription drugs to fix things like high blood pressure, cholesterol, or weight gain. And some people cannot be without these. However, others of us could make better lifestyle choices to avoid feeding the pharmaceutical industry.

I want to be healthy as I grow old so no one else has to take care of me. I want to be independent and strong. This is the other main reason I treat my body as kindly as possible.

Find out how to keep your body happy in the chapters that follow.

(As I said earlier, I'm not a doctor, so be sure to consult your doctor before starting any new fitness routine!)

FUEL YOUR BODY RIGHT

The term "Garbage in. Garbage out." is how you should think about the things you put into your body. Your health starts with the things you use to fuel your body. Some things provide temporary energy (like caffeine and sugar), but fresh, whole foods can create lasting health and cellular strength.

Sugar is one of the worst substances for your body. When your body processes sugar, it uses up a bunch of water and dehydrates you. That can lead to headaches, lethargy, and other uncomfortable symptoms. But also, sugar is shown to cause disease in your body and to be addictive like a drug.

Any of us are susceptible to disease or illness, and some of the determination of whether those diseases take hold and prosper in our body is our health, including our immune system health. Things like sugar, alcohol, excessive red meat, and smoking weaken our immune response and make it more likely that diseases, viruses, and other maladies will afflict us.

The best foods for you are the ones with limited, recognizable ingredients. The best foods overall are those in their natural state, unprocessed - like apples or brown rice or chickpeas.

I know it can feel intimidating to cook with fresh vegetables and whole-ingredient foods if you are not accustomed to doing that. You also may not have a good place near you to buy fresh produce. A farmers market or farm stand is the best place to get fruits and veggies because most of them come straight from the farm. When your produce has dirt on it, it's fresh!

If your city or town doesn't have a farmers market, call up your local officials and tell them you want one. Have your friends call, too! Start a movement for fresh, local fruits and veggies.

Many people just want to eat what they want to eat, and that might work for a while. But eventually, your eating habits catch up with you. I've had more than a few friends suffer heart attacks in their 40s due to poor diet. If you're lucky, you survive and are given a second chance to live a healthier life.

The more fresh veggies you eat and the more ways you learn to cook them, the more they will become something you can't live without… and the happier and healthier your body will be.

Don't forget that being unhealthy is expensive. More doctor visits. More prescriptions. More trips to the ER. More money for capitalists. The more you can stay away from doctors, the more money you'll have in your pocket. Give your money to farmers so you don't have to give way more of it to the pharmaceutical companies.

Small farmers are the opposite of capitalists. They are our neighbors who provide us with fresh, healthy food that hasn't traveled a long distance to get to us. If we're lucky, they practice organic farming methods, but even if they don't, it's still beneficial to eat fresh, local fruits, vegetables, and other produce.

It's fairly easy to start off eating more veggies. There are three basic things you can do with them: saute them, boil/steam them, or roast/bake them. Add olive oil at the beginning and a small amount of salt at the end, and throw them over a reasonable portion of pasta or brown rice. Season to your taste.

Talk to your local farmers about what's in season and what kind of farming practices they use. Ask them what that vegetable is that you don't recognize. They might even be able to suggest how to cook it or point you to a recipe.

We only get this one body, and we owe it to ourselves to give it the best fuel that we can.

MOVE IT OR LOSE IT

Our body is an amazing machine. All of our parts and organs are in symbiotic relationships with each other. Our organs process our inputs and turn them into outputs. Our bones, muscles, tendons, and skin hold everything together and coordinate our movements.

We are living miracles!

But our body is something that needs to be maintained just like our other prized possessions. If it sits on the shelf too long, it will get rusty, stiff, and creaky.

When we're younger, we're often more active. But if not, it's harder to learn good habits later. When we get older, our lives often become more sedentary. Along with slowing your metabolism and causing stiff muscles, sitting too much can increase your risk of death from cardiovascular disease and cancer.

It's important, as we get older, to keep our muscles, tendons, and joints strong, moving and healthy. If we don't, we risk injuring ourselves. The older we get, the more prone we will be to injury and the kinder and gentler we'll need to be with our bodies. Overworking your body can be as detrimental as underworking it.

Many people who played sports in high school or who have been involved in high-impact activities have damage to their knees, hips, or shoulders. Now is the time to take good care of ourselves.

Capitalism would love to sell you products and services to help keep your body strong and healthy. Some of them might be things you really need, like a time-tested supplement or some great walking shoes. But mostly, you can stay healthy without spending a lot of money. A sturdy bicycle and a good pair of supportive walking or running shoes will go a long way if properly cared for.

Often, the reason we don't take care of our bodies is that we feel tired or strapped for time – two side effects of capitalism. But putting off stretching and exercise will only compound things. Our sore knee can turn into a knee replacement. Our muscle weakness can become total body lethargy.

The worst thing we can do is make our older age a time of inactivity and discomfort. If we make it to that place, we want to be vibrant and still able to have the adventures that keep us young at heart and feed our joy.

It's terrible that capitalism sees our health as something to make money from. It's terrible that we are told we need to spend a bunch of money in order to live a healthy life. It can seem tempting to click on all the ads that claim to make us younger, healthier, fitter, and more active. But there is often a high cost to those ads that would burden us with another detrimental thing as we grow old: financial stress. And many times, their solutions are not as advertised.

Always ask yourself, "How could I accomplish this same thing differently in a way that would cost me a lot less?"

Creativity is the death of capitalism. When we get creative and think outside the confines of capitalism about how to reach our goals (whether it's getting healthy or taking a trip), we are giving the middle finger to capitalism.

A great way to stay excited about exercise is to have several things you like to do: biking, walking, yoga (free on YouTube), gym workouts (there are some cheap memberships if that's for you, but don't get caught with a gym membership you never use), hiking, kayaking (you can rent one), etc.

This keeps things fresh and gives you options for moving your body.

PRACTICE HEALING AND RESTING

Capitalism has us working frantically, with full-time jobs, part-time jobs, side hustles, and everything in between. We're busy trying to monetize every part of our life, from our house to our driveway to our own car.

Experts seem to agree that people who don't take breaks or vacations are actually less productive than those who do.[9]

And besides, we deserve to rest. We deserve to stop. In fact, if we don't choose to stop and rest, our body often chooses that for us. Except instead of time to relax and regroup, our body throws us into sickness - usually by causing our weakened immune system to catch a cold, the flu, or even a major illness.

We don't need to think about work every moment of the day. Even if we are in a bad financial situation, there is a tremendous benefit to scheduling time to decompress.

Downtime from work inspires our creativity. It's nearly impossible to be creative without space in our minds and schedules, and creativity can help us find solutions to our capitalist problems.

As I mention in a later chapter, our spending choices sometimes require us to work more. Use downtime to examine areas where you could cut expenses to cut your need to be constantly hustling. You can also use downtime to decide if skills training might help you find a job that pays more so you can hustle less. Finding a job that is unionized means you'll have the power to fight for fair pay and working conditions.

Some of us simply think that we should be working all the time. Maybe we're modeling our parents' behavior, or we've bought into societal norms and pressures about work. But there's no prize for over-working. If we stand still for a moment, we might realize how unhappy we are. Overworking fills every moment so we can't examine the issues in our lives.

Overworking is also a way to justify impulsive purchases that feel good at the moment but don't add any lasting joy to our lives.

Rest and healing can look like:

- spending time in nature
- sitting in your favorite chair with a cup of tea/coffee
- meeting a friend for coffee
- spending time with a cherished family member
- journaling
- taking a long, hot bath or shower
- doing an art project you've been putting off

AVOID EXCESS

Willpower is a tricky thing. I believe it is something you can cultivate and strengthen, but it is difficult for many people.

The ultimate key to having willpower is self-awareness. If we can learn to recognize when we are heading toward excess (or already in it), we can make a decision to pull back on whatever we are over-using.

In this stressful, capitalistic society, excess is encouraged. We see countless ads every day for food, alcohol, baubles, and all sorts of products and services. We see these ads over and over again, and sometimes, they get into our psyche and fuel our cravings. But many of the things advertised are poisons: alcohol, cigarettes, sugary drinks, fatty foods, and junk food laden with chemicals and preservatives. We're being asked to pay to make ourselves less healthy. It's silly when you think about it.

Many people in many places drink alcohol every single day. When you spend time with them, it seems normal, but then you realize you're drinking every single day, and you don't want to do that for health and financial reasons.

Willpower is the ability to control how much of anything you buy and/or consume. Many people are impulsive shoppers because it is such an ingrained part of American society. We are often referred to as "consumers." That infers that we're just a mechanism by which capitalism makes money. But you don't need to be a consumer. You can be a conscientious person who makes smart choices.

Obviously, we need to buy things, but we should be mindful and not repeatedly purchase things because of ads.

So many companies push their very unhealthy food at us in stores and online. An occasional treat is nice, but sugar has addictive qualities that can make us crave it. We might not realize this is happening or that we're eating too much of it until it starts to make us feel bad.

Willpower is the self-awareness to know if we're consuming too much of a particular thing (food, alcohol, news, social media, unnecessary purchases) and the ability to correct course.

Cultivating willpower is a part of self-care. Over-consuming will not make us healthy or prosperous. Learning how to moderate our behavior keeps us moving along without as many stressful ups and downs in our progress. We all get off track sometimes, but if we learn how to correct course before too much damage is done, we'll be able to avoid any long-term issues.

GET COMFORTABLE WITH YOUR SEXUALITY

Does this have to do with capitalism? If joy is the antidote to capitalism, then yes, it does.

Some of us grew up in a household where sex was never talked about, and we learned to be ashamed of our bodies and our sexual inclinations no matter what they were.

It's difficult to have a satisfying sex life if you don't know anything about your body or how to make yourself feel good.

My advice is to learn about the things that make your body feel good. Do them to yourself (if possible) in a safe environment. Go to a reputable sex shop and buy some toys to experiment with.

Then, not only can you pleasure yourself when no one else is around, but you can guide your partner into doing the same. (And there's no shame in using sex toys with a partner.)

Sometimes, we don't get pleasure out of sex because we don't tell the other person what we need. But we don't have to make them guess. Thoughtful partners want you to enjoy the sex you're having together. You should want them to enjoy it, too.

What you like about sex or how you like to have sex may change over the years, so keep communicating. Sex is largely about two things: communication and trust. That's it.

Any sort of liberation, including sexual liberation, is an affront to capitalism.

LEARN WHAT YOUR BODY IS CAPABLE OF

Our bodies are incredible machines! We should try new things with our bodies. Stretch it in new ways. Learn how it can move.

There are so many muscles in your body that you likely ignore.

Never tried rock climbing? Find your nearest climbing gym. Want to build your core muscles? Buy some rollerblades (and plenty of padding), or try stand-up paddle boarding. Remember that you can often rent (or borrow) equipment instead of buying.

Tai chi is a great muscle builder. Yoga is great for stretching. Both involve calm, healing movements.

Most yoga or tai chi studios are local small businesses, but you can also use free resources like YouTube to learn and practice these skills. Just ignore any ads so as not to feed the capitalists.

You can build stamina with some bike riding.

Your body is an amazing creation, and you should explore all the things it can do.

FIGHT FOR BODILY AUTONOMY

> "Data from the Centers for Disease Control and Prevention (CDC) clearly show that pregnancy is a condition that can kill you."[10]
>
> Dr. Sarah Horvath, Penn State University's Hershey Medical Center

Women, in particular, have historically had their bodily autonomy stolen from them. Men have objectified and assaulted them. The government has tried to legislate what they can and can't do when they're pregnant. Women often don't have the ability or the right to determine how their body is treated by others.

Whenever possible, you should fight for women's bodily autonomy, which includes the right to privacy in their healthcare decisions. Women, and only women, should decide what's right for them, including whether they have an abortion.

What do abortion rights have to do with capitalism? I'm glad you asked. Abortion is a very controversial issue that conservative leaders use to fearmonger their base into voting for them so they (the elected officials) can serve their corporate overlords. These leaders don't really care about abortion. It is simply a heated issue they use to rile people up. Are you one of those people?

But what about the liberals/Democrats? They're passionate about abortion, too. What if I told you the Democrats also use this issue to rouse their base and conveniently never do anything substantive about it, even when they have a majority in Congress? But they still campaign on promises to protect it, which largely go unfulfilled. I guess they hope people won't notice as they stay focused on trying to convince you how bad the Republicans are.

As you might have noticed, capitalism is run mostly by the patriarchy (men). By putting more and more controls on women's bodies and thus their economic security, insecure men who are part of the patriarchy can continue to feel like they're in control. (More on them later.)

If our capitalist society truly cared about women, the U.S. would not have the highest maternal mortality rate in the developed world at 22.3.[11] The maternal mortality rate is how many women out of every 100,000 women who give birth to a living baby are dying during that birth. This is a measure of how well we take care of women when they are bringing life into this world. For Black women in America, it's even worse at 49.5.[12] In contrast, the maternal mortality rate for having an abortion in the first trimester (which is when 90% of all abortions happen) is only 1 in 100,000.[13] In European countries, the maternal mortality rate is generally between 2 and 12, while even Eastern European countries like Romania have a rate of only 10.[14] That means it's twice as safe to give birth in Romania as it is in the United States. How do you feel about that?

Forcing a woman to give birth in the U.S. puts her in over 20 times as much danger as allowing her to have an abortion if she chooses.[15] Why would you want your lover, friend, sister, or aunt to risk death for a pregnancy they don't want? That's hella selfish.

No matter what your political or religious affiliation is, the women you know deserve to make their private decisions in private and not be put at risk of physical harm because of the demands of a politician and not the advice of their doctor. As someone who loves them, you should help protect them. It's never about abortion for political leaders. It's always about them holding onto power and helping make more profit for capitalists.

RESOURCES

BOOKS:

The Body Keeps the Score by Bessel van der Kolk
The Wisdom of Your Body by Hillary L. McBride

HOMEWORK:

Buy a vegetable you've never cooked before, find a recipe to cook it, and enjoy a new culinary experience.

If you are able, take one whole day without an agenda. Do whatever you want, including nothing at all. Choose activities that feed your body and mind. Only do things that feel nurturing.

RELATIONSHIPS

INTRO

"At the risk of seeming ridiculous, let me say that the true revolutionary is guided by a great feeling of love. It is impossible to think of a genuine revolutionary lacking this quality."[16]

Che Guevara

In this section, we'll explore the vital role of human connections in creating a joyful and fulfilling life. In a world driven by capitalist ideas that often prioritize individual success and material wealth over genuine human bonds, it's crucial to remember that much of our happiness stems from the quality of our relationships. Whether it's family, friends, or community, the people we surround ourselves with can profoundly impact our well-being and resilience against the pressures of a consumer-driven society.

In this section, we'll delve into the importance of nurturing relationships that bring joy, support, and growth. We'll discuss how to identify and cultivate meaningful connections, communicate effectively, and build a diverse and supportive social network.

By focusing on authentic interactions and mutual respect, we can create a strong community that not only enhances our personal joy but also empowers us to resist the isolating effects of capitalism.

SURROUND YOURSELF WITH GOOD PEOPLE

They say, "Birds of a feather flock together," so what do your bird friends say about you? How do you choose the people you spend the most time with? Do your friends challenge you to be your best self? Or are they people you sit around with to complain and make excuses? Are they encouragers or discouragers? Are they people you can be honest with? Do they bring you joy?

"Good people" are those you can trust. They are people who are reliable when you need them.

When you find good people to be part of your circle, you have to nurture those relationships. You have to be a "good person," too, so they will feel loved and appreciated.

Your social circle should include people you respect and ones who can teach you things. Having friends of different age groups is valuable - those older and younger than you have wisdom and knowledge you don't have. It's also valuable to befriend people of different skin colors, backgrounds, nationalities, and sexual orientations. Everyone has something to teach us.

You should have a variety of people you seek support from (and give support to). This lessens the burden on any one person and gives any of them the opportunity to opt out of providing comfort to you if their own life is feeling overwhelming at the time. We should never expect people to unconditionally be there for us. It's not realistic and doesn't take into account the many variables at play in each person's life.

You can find community in your family, your friends, your neighborhood, your soccer club, your church, or the parents club at your child's school. And while you might have an online community, you need to also be surrounded by good people who are close to you geographically. They are the ones who will be there when you need to borrow their lawnmower, and they're the ones you can loan your truck to when they need to move a mattress.

This kind of material support bonds us together, helps us save money, and makes us feel more secure when bad things happen. It is antithetical to ideas pushed by capitalism.

MAKE AUTHENTIC CONNECTIONS

Today's world can be very superficial. We see images of people on social media that don't necessarily tell us anything substantial or meaningful about them. Often, it is about "image," and "likes," and "followers." For all we know, these people are smiling for selfies while enduring painful and challenging conditions in their lives.

Many of the people we encounter during the week are not true connections but only acquaintances… or the store checkout clerk.

We are often too focused on work or survival to have time to nurture true friendships or deep connections.

Because of this, we often form advantageous or opportunistic relationships with people. We might not even realize we're doing this, and we might even think this is normal. If you find yourself unsure of what you bring to a perceived friendship, you might ask yourself if it's really a friendship at all or just you spending time with the person for some benefit. (Their pool, car, money, connections, etc.) Or maybe you laden them with all your emotional issues without reciprocating.

Authentic connections are made when we listen to people and make them feel truly heard, when we try to understand them and what motivates them, and when we try to contribute positively to their lives.

We don't have to be best friends to have an authentic connection, and we don't have to have everything in common. In fact, making authentic connections with people with whom you don't have everything in common is a great way to stick it to capitalism. The more "different" connections you have, the more empathy you will have toward people and the less you will buy into capitalism's attempts to divide us. You will also learn interesting new things that you couldn't learn by only spending time with people like you. Not the least of those things are new points of view. Try connecting with people who have different: ages, ethnicities, skin colors, nationalities, sexual orientations, professions, incomes, and interests.

You will gain so much value in your life by doing that.

LEARN TO COMMUNICATE

Good communication is essential if we want to have joy-filled relationships, and joy-filled relationships can help us cope with the negative impacts of capitalism.

Learning to communicate is about learning to say what you mean, feel, and need. It's also about listening.

Confrontation can be a scary thing to lean into, but knowing how to be honest and have productive conversations and arguments is a skill that will add incredible value to your life. It will help you in your personal relationships and help you stand up to those more powerful than you.

Often, we get little direction from our families on how to communicate in a healthy way. In that case, we owe it to ourselves to do all we can to learn, even if it's ugly at first. Learning to communicate better liberated me from carrying around unexpressed feelings. Expressing myself when I've been disrespected unburdens me from feeling unheard and unseen. It's also fair to the other person (especially if they're someone you care about) to let them know that you're upset with them and why. They deserve that from you.

So, how can you become a better communicator?

Before you communicate, think about what you're communicating and why. Do you need to tell someone you don't like their outfit? Or that they have this little habit you don't like? You shouldn't simply complain about everything in the name of "honesty," but you can bring to the forefront important issues that may impact you in a negative way, like unkind, disrespectful, or abusive behavior.

You deserve to be heard. You deserve to have honest conversations with people you love. The same goes for people you work or volunteer with. You deserve to have people around you who you can trust with your feelings and needs.

Communicating with your partner is the key to making a romantic relationship work. You should be able to say the things that are bothering you in a loving way and trust that your partner will accept and appreciate your feelings. You should both have the same goal: a loving, honest relationship.

Learning to communicate is often about saying things in a way that is not threatening to the other person. I don't believe in "brutal honesty." I think being kind in your criticism goes a long way toward truly being heard. But it's also about owning that your feelings should not be dictated by someone else. There is a balance between making other people responsible for your feelings (they're not) and wanting them to care how their actions affect you.

You should address issues right away when they arise instead of letting them fester. You can take time to think about how you will address the issue, but you shouldn't wait too long so the other person will still have a fresh memory of what happened. They are probably not thinking about it the way you are.

Communicating is not always about agreeing. It's often about listening to the other person so you can understand their point of view. That doesn't mean convincing the other person that you're right (or being convinced that you're wrong). The end result should be harmony in the relationship, whatever kind of relationship that is. This concept seems almost impossible to understand in our current ultra-polarized world, but we must get back to this balance of accepting that we can all be different and still live harmoniously.

Communicating removes the need to make assumptions. Confused about something? Just ask. It's that easy. Want the other person to know something? Just tell them. See how that works? Don't make them guess how you feel, and don't pretend to feel a way you don't.

If you feel you're in a relationship of any kind with someone you can't freely communicate with honestly, then it might not be a healthy relationship for you.

Examine the communication style you have with various people in your life. Is it open? Does it feel healthy? Do you feel the person is someone you can have a healthy conflict with?

It's OK to remove people from your life or spend less time with people who you can't talk freely with.

The other part of communication is listening, and it's something you can practice. The next time a friend comes to you with a concern, listen to them in silence. Then, reflect back to them what you heard and ask them if that is accurate. Often, communication breaks down between the mouth of one person and the mental filters of the other.

Learn to hear what the person is really saying, not what you interpret them to be saying. Ask questions for clarification.

Honesty and good listening skills can help keep all your relationships strong. And having strong, joyful relationships can help us thrive in this capitalist hellscape.

DON'T BE SO JUDGY

At some point in our lives, we all judge other people. Why do we do this? Part of it is insecurity. Part of it is trying to fit into a social group. But we all do it.

This is another way our system of capitalism tries to divide us. It tries to convince us that we are better than THOSE people. The ones over there. The ones that are different than us. (Except they're really not that different than us.) Why do THOSE people get to have things that we don't get to have? ("How did HE afford that house?")

Judging people is one way we connect with others who share the same insecurities. It can seem innocent, but it reinforces our negative ideas about other people. Most of the time, the things we judge are petty and have nothing to do with what kind of person our target actually is. ("Look at her hair! It's so awful.")

Resisting the urge to judge others (either in our minds or out loud to others) helps us reconcile our own ideas about ourselves. We should ask ourselves, "Why do I feel this way? Why do I care so much about this? Am I projecting? Is my judgment connected to something I don't like or accept about myself? Is this worth caring, thinking, and talking about?"

Sometimes, we judge out of jealousy because we feel like someone else is doing so much better than us. But we often don't see the entirety of their situation, and if we did, we might feel more grateful for the circumstances of our own lives and stop adding negativity to theirs. Maybe they're going through cancer treatment or have just lost a loved one. Maybe they recently got laid off from their job or had a $500 rent increase they're struggling to afford. Do you really need to add your petty judgment to their existing problems? (Remember what we just learned about empathy?)

Judging others is about wanting to gain a sense of superiority over them when, deep down, we really don't feel superior at all. It's often about trying to find ways that we're better than them because we feel bad about some aspect of our own life.

Part of not judging people is learning to be OK with our own life despite its challenges. It's knowing that other people are not the cause of our problems but that it's easy for us to direct our frustration at them. ("I'm struggling with paying my bills, but that person is getting FREE FOOD from food stamps.")

Capitalism wants us to be jealous. It wants us to fill that hole of jealousy with products that might make us feel like we're better off than we are and better than that other person. Did they just buy a big house that we wish we could have? Capitalism will sell us a bigger house! But maybe we forgot to notice that we are a single-income household, and that person has two incomes in their household. Whoops! Now we're in over our heads.

They have a super nice newer car. Capitalism will sell us a new car, too. Except the interest rates have gone up almost 3%, and now we're paying way more. Whoops! Look where our jealousy got us.

People even judge food stamp recipients because they sometimes buy a steak. Imagine being jealous of someone with less money than you!

Capitalists love your judgyness. If you keep it up, you'll make them rich. But you won't be rich. You might look like you're rich, but you'll be saddled with debt and extra stress from trying to keep up with the materialism of those around you. But don't worry, capitalism will try to "help" you with that, too. (By offering you a high-interest personal loan, a monthly subscription to an expensive gym, or a luxury vacation in the Bahamas.)

Instead of judging others, pay attention to your own life and how you can keep it filled with joy.

DON'T STEREOTYPE GROUPS

"Too often, we judge other groups by their worst examples - while judging ourselves by our best intentions. And this has strained our bonds of understanding and common purpose."[17]

George W. Bush

In our search for easy ways to understand the world, it is tempting to characterize the members of racial, ethnic, cultural, or political groups using homogeneous terms.

The problem is that this ignores the complex nature of humans. Yes, people have things in common with their respective groups, but each individual is so much more than that. They have autonomous thoughts, interests, hobbies, beliefs, and longings.

Even groups that seem inherently bad on the surface contain people who are complex and have redeeming qualities. When we look at a group and not at the individual members, we miss opportunities to see their different motivations and aspirations.

When we stereotype, it is easier for us to have animosity toward people because we can't see their individual humanity. In fact, this is how we learn to see people simply as "other"… and something to be frightened of or repelled by.

Making us stereotype and fear certain groups is a great way for capitalists to sell us a new house in a gated community, dangerous weapons, or a fancy alarm system. But you do not need to succumb to the fear of other people. The world is not full of bogeymen waiting to kill you. First off, you're really not that important. Secondly, you're much more likely to die from heart disease, so I suggest you eat less red meat, don't spend too much time sitting, and take regular walks around your neighborhood. Ironically, this will not only make you healthier, but it will make your neighborhood safer.

Let's talk about race. According to science, there is no such thing as biological or genetic race. Race (especially the concept of "black" and "white") is bullshit made up by capitalism and used during the time of slavery in the United States. By creating a distinction between "white" and "black," a hierarchy was created that was used to make us look down on others. Those considered "white" would enforce this system of hierarchy because even poor "whites" were considered better than "blacks" of any economic standing.[18]

There's definitely no "white" race or nationality because "white" isn't a thing. There is no common culture for "white" people. Some seemingly "white" people are of English, Irish or Scottish descent. Some are Scandinavian or from Baltic countries. Some people who are Chinese, Japanese, Mexican, African American, or Indian are considered "white," depending on the shade of their skin. Frankly, the only people with truly white skin are albinos. Most everyone else has some level of pigment in their skin, so the use of the term "white" is neither literally nor figuratively accurate. People who are perceived as "white" in America receive the most privileges of any group. They are not hindered by the prejudices experienced by other groups.

My use of the term Black in this book is due to the fact that people perceived as "black" in our country are treated a certain way regardless of where they are from. Black Americans who are descendants of African slaves do share a common culture and history, beginning with their kidnapping from their home countries and transport to America. We know there is a historical precedent of racism against African Americans, but because people of many other nationalities look "black" in appearance, they are often subject to the same prejudice and mistreatment. Therefore, I use the term Black to designate anyone who falls under this umbrella.[19] A relevant example of this is Kamala Harris. While her nationality is Indian and Jamaican from her parents, most people who look at her don't know that and simply see a Black woman. Because some of society has prejudices against Black women, they immediately apply all those to her regardless of her background.

Even though race doesn't technically exist, people still perceive that it does, and so we must confront the racism and racial discrimination that this creates.

It will help you to be less ignorant about all of this if you educate yourself about the history of slavery, civil rights, and racism in the U.S. By doing this, you can avoid perpetuating racist stereotypes and widening the imaginary differences between human beings.

Let's talk about political parties. Unfortunately, there are only two parties in the U.S. with any sort of power at the moment, and they don't fully encompass the range of beliefs and ideals held by the American people.

There are registered Democrats and Republicans who believe a wide range of things outside their political party's platform. (Thank goodness!) But we often find it expedient to simply apply all of the worst things about their party to them as individuals.

However, your fellow voters are not the enemy. For the most part, they are just trying to live their lives and be happy and healthy, just like you. They've been subjected to the same capitalist propaganda you have, and they are subject to the same harmful effects of capitalism as you.

Finding a common enemy is a way candidates try to bring people together to get elected and also to distract voters from the shitty things they're doing (or good things they should be doing but are not doing). Democrats and Republicans both do it.

But it also builds insurmountable walls within our society and polarizes our nation in a way that hurts us all. No one wins that game except politicians, big corporations, and the military-industrial complex.

I'm sure you're seeing a pattern: division is bad for us but great for people trying to make money off that division. Anything we can be disgruntled about is a way for capitalism to open the door to receive the contents of our wallets.

We should know that however we feel about other groups of people, they may also feel the same things about us. It's a vicious cycle of ignorance and manipulation. We should not allow ourselves to be influenced by the will of capitalism. We can learn to see through it and treat our fellow Americans like we're on the same team.

One thing capitalism cannot do is force us to be unkind or cruel. That is a decision that we alone can make. We control our own behavior and have no one else to blame when we act badly.

If you think you may be stereotyping people, join a local group whose members are intercultural and diverse. Spend time around people who aren't like you and toward whom you might hold stereotypes.

We hear a lot of stereotypes, but we don't have to adopt them. Meet people. Learn their story. Or just mind your own damn business and assume the best about people.

SEE THE GOOD IN PEOPLE

Often, we are very quick to judge someone as "bad" because of a particular thing about them that we don't like, something that is only a fraction of who they really are. Often, we are listening to the media (part of the capitalist system) tell us what should be considered "bad."

But what if we decided to pay attention to the good things about people instead of the bad? What if we assumed that most people are mostly good?

I believe most people are good. Therefore, I trust that most people aren't going to harm me. Because I believe this, I have traveled all over the world by myself and walked around strange and wonderful places without accompaniment. If I thought most people were bad, I wouldn't have done that.

Obviously, there are certain people who are less safe in certain places. This isn't an invitation to put yourself in danger. But it is an invitation to examine your thoughts about people, why you think that way about them, if there's any solid evidence to back up your ideas, and if maybe you need to bring it down a notch.

I try to find the good in even the people who are considered very bad by most of society. I believe almost all humans have an innate goodness. If humans have an innate goodness but are not acting "good," then there is a reason for that. Maybe they are experiencing mental, emotional, or financial pain. Many people don't know how to deal with painful feelings in a healthy way. They may act out with harmful behaviors because they don't have the resources to find better answers or don't have an example of better ways to behave.

Sometimes, it's easy to see the good in people, but we choose not to because we cling to our incorrect or incomplete beliefs about them. We can take responsibility for our thoughts and feelings, though. We can educate ourselves about misconceptions and choose to focus on the positive.

SET HEALTHY BOUNDARIES

Many of us, when we were young, were taught about manners. We were taught how to be polite to others, to help people, to be kind to our elders, and other rules of etiquette that made us into nice people.

But somewhere along the way, some of us came to believe that we had to forfeit our own happiness for that of others. We may have kept saying "Yes" to everyone at all times. Then, one day, we woke up and realized we had said "Yes" too many times and were feeling overwhelmed and under-appreciated. Some of us took huge burdens upon ourselves that we could not manage because we kept saying yes without regard to our own capacity.

In being nice, we weren't being kind to ourselves. We were being agreeable. We were avoiding conflict. But we were also setting unrealistic expectations of how much we could really do for others while still taking care of ourselves in a way that was sustainable.

Despite what we might tell ourselves when trying to feel like a hero, martyrdom is not an attractive quality. No one who cares about you wants you to give too much of yourself for them. If they do, they are not a kind person.

Even if you have free time, it's OK to say no to someone who wants you to fill it with their needs. Even if you care about them. You're allowed to have downtime to recharge.

There is nothing at all wrong with helping people. You should give back in some way, whether by being there for a relative, by volunteering, or through activism. But you don't have to do those things at the cost of your mental or physical well-being.

But it's not just requests for help that you can decline. You can also say no when your friends invite you out, and you just don't want to. You can say no (in a diplomatic way) when your boss asks you to work beyond your capacity. You can say no when someone asks you out romantically, and you're not into it. You can even say no to a child trying to sell you Girl Scout cookies! (Just be polite in your rejection.)

What might be extra surprising to you is that you don't need to explain yourself if you don't want to do something or don't have the capacity. You can simply say, "No, thank you." You don't owe anyone an explanation (although you might prepare something for your boss or client).

Some of us have been so programmed to say yes that we think not wanting to do something makes us a bad person. Just imagine! Don't we get a say in our own thoughts and feelings about something?! Yes, yes, we do.

Setting boundaries is not just about saying "No," though. It's about creating rules to help other people know how we'd like to be treated. We can tell people what kind of behaviors we will and will not tolerate in our lives.

Boundaries are meant to teach people how to respect you. They should be reasonable. Boundaries should be rules that define who you are. What will we tolerate? Where are our limits? What do we insist on to keep our lives joyful?

Capitalism is designed to take advantage of people who were raised to be agreeable. Salespeople can be aggressive and appeal to our innate politeness. After a window salesman refused to leave my house without my repeated insistence, I set a boundary that I would not pull the trigger on any major purchase on the day it was presented to me. Salespeople know that if you have time to think about it, you will often change your mind. That's why they push so hard for you to complete the sale right away. I tell each salesperson my "sleep on it" rule upfront so they know their aggressive tactics will not work on me.

We can make these kinds of rules/boundaries in all areas of our lives, from relationships to work to social interactions.

And remember, some people in your life may not like these rules because they benefited from you not having them. You will need to assess who supports you in demanding a reasonable amount of respect for your time and energy.

NOT EVERYONE WILL LIKE YOU AND THAT'S OK

Social media has created a space that's geared toward competition for people's attention and "likes."

Because we aren't always our authentic selves on social media, we sometimes start controversial arguments. Other people get triggered by our blunt or outrageous posts, and then we might get called out, unfriended, or even blocked by them. In fact, the social media algorithm is geared toward this controversy because when you engage in it, capitalists get more ad revenue from your interactions. This is part of the outrage machine, which will be discussed later on.

Some people are just hellbent on misinterpreting what you say and being contrarian. That's their entertainment, and it's all a game to them.

Sometimes, people get angry at even the most innocent things we say because they interpret them through their own lens of experiences. Some people will never like anything we say because of our ideologies or beliefs. Or they might just not like the color of our hair.

I'm here to tell you that that's OK.

You will probably not like everyone in the world, and they are not going to like you either. Some personalities just don't mix. This is important to remember as we navigate our opposition to capitalism. We can be on the same team against the ruling class even if we don't like each other or disagree on other things. In fact, we must learn to do that if we're to make any change in this world.

Whatever the reason someone doesn't like you, it's not worth your time or energy to try to convince someone, especially a stranger, to like you.

We don't have to make everyone like us. And in fact, you can't "make" someone like you. People have all sorts of reasons why they might not like us, and it's not for us to decipher. It is not your responsibility to make everyone happy, and it is a big waste of your precious time, love, and energy to try.

As I mentioned earlier, we want to surround ourselves with people we respect and trust. You don't have to let everyone into your inner circle, and you definitely don't have to spend time around people you don't really like.

Being secure and having confidence means that you can be OK if someone else decides they don't like you. What matters is that you continue to be the best person you can be and not worry about the haters.

LEARN TO ENJOY YOUR OWN COMPANY

Relationships of all kinds are great. Whether with family, friends, or romantic partners, they provide companionship, love, and affection.

However, I was raised with the notion that to be "whole" as a person, I must have a romantic partner, preferably a husband. I was taught to fear the idea of being "alone." I was led to believe that not only did being single mean I was undesirable but also that I would fail miserably if I tried to make it through life all by my helpless self.

Therefore, the idea of being alone felt terrifying to me. It was something to be avoided at all costs.

Then, the inevitable happened. In my desperate attempts to escape the perceived horror of being alone, I ended up in a Very Bad Relationship. It was a psychologically confusing relationship, but what wasn't confusing was how Very Bad it was. I struggled to admit to myself how Very Bad the situation was until I finally felt like I was going crazy and got the heck out of there.

Fortunately, some very good things came out of the Very Bad Relationship.

After six months of grief over allowing myself to end up in that relationship, I began to unpack the false narrative of what it means to be alone. As I progressed on my healing journey, I began to enjoy living alone and being single. I felt proud of the business I was building and the lifestyle it was affording me. Every new accomplishment achieved on my own brought with it an increasing sense of self-confidence.

At age 51, I can't imagine not having ample alone time to do the things I'm passionate about or to just sit and drink tea with my cat in my lap. I value my own space and being able to sit quietly in it without being bothered by any of the demons I used to harbor.

Having a feeling of contentedness is worth more than anything capitalism can sell you. In fact, this feeling of inner peace causes me to continue to simplify my life from material things because I see that none of them can bring me the joy that simply getting right with myself did.

Learning to enjoy your own company is not just for those who are single or living alone. It also helps create space for family, friends, and partners to grow and evolve.

TALK TO STRANGERS

Enjoying your own company is only part of finding joy. There is also joy in getting to know others.

As I mentioned earlier, talking to strangers can help break down stereotypes. It can reveal to us that people we don't know are mostly just like us, despite the stories we have in our heads.

With the advent of the internet, people are much more isolated from each other, even if it sort of feels like we're being "social."

The internet is not real life, though. Real life is outside your dwelling or office. It's on the street and in the coffee shops. Aren't you curious about that guy with the beautiful tie? Or the woman with the baby? Who are they? What is their life like? You're both standing in the same line for movie tickets. Why don't you say hello and strike up a conversation?

Are you traveling? Why not ask some of the locals what it's like to live there? Do they worry about crime? Do they have kids in school? What's their favorite local restaurant?

Talking to strangers is its own education. Especially if we talk to people who might fall outside our ethnicity, religion, political views, sexual orientation, or gender. I grew up in a very small town, and I was always hungry to talk to anyone with a different experience than me. Getting different perspectives on life helps us be more accepting of others and prevents capitalism from keeping us divided.

RESOURCES

BOOKS:

The Power of Strangers by Joe Keohane
So You Want to Talk About Race by Ijeoma Oluo
How to Love by Thich Nhat Hahn
Nonviolent Communication by Marshall Rosenberg

HOMEWORK:

What local organizations can you join to spend time around a diverse array of people?

Are there boundaries you should set in your life? How can you go about setting and enforcing them?

WORK

INTRO

> *"I want to say, in all seriousness, that a great deal of harm is being done in the modern world by the belief in the virtuousness of work, and that the road to happiness and prosperity lies in an organized diminution of work."*[20]
>
> Bertrand Russell

In this section, we'll challenge the conventional wisdom that our lives should be dominated by our jobs. Here, we explore the idea that work should support your life, not consume it. This section is about finding balance, cultivating joy, and ensuring that your job serves as a means to live your life on your own terms.

We'll delve into the pitfalls of hustle culture, the importance of building practical skills, and ways to redefine success on your own terms. Whether you're looking to escape the grind or simply seeking a more fulfilling work-life balance, this section offers insights to help you navigate your career without losing yourself in the process. Let's redefine what it means to work and live well in a world that often demands the opposite.

While some of this chapter is directed at folks who are self-employed or freelancers, most of the same advice can apply to those working a traditional job.

WORK TO LIVE. DON'T LIVE TO WORK.

> *"Decide how you want to live and then see what you can do to make a living WITHIN that way of life."*[21]
> Hunter S. Thompson

Our life does not need to revolve around our job or profession. Many people's identities get lost in their work, but it doesn't have to be that way. There is more to you than just your job.

While I love what I do for a living, I do not get up in the morning thinking my passion is to work. My passion is to travel. I work so that I can do the things I love. I work so that I can live the lifestyle I want to live, which includes a flexible schedule and the ability to work from home and from anywhere.

I don't work for the sake of work, although I do enjoy creating things as part of my job. But my job is what allows me to live the kind of life I want to live.

If I could travel regularly without working, I would do that.

I know this is not as easy for some people as it is for others because of the damage capitalism has done to society, but we shouldn't have to sell our souls for money. We should be paid fairly and have enough work/life balance to feel fulfilled and rested.

Unions are a way for workers to band together and fight for livable conditions and pay from their employers. If you work for a sizable company, consider doing some research into starting or joining a union. We can also fight for fair pay and decent jobs for everyone on a local and national level by pressuring candidates and elected officials.

To any extent we can, we should not let our jobs take over our lives. We should nurture all the different facets of ourselves, from the artist to the fisherman.

AVOID HUSTLE CULTURE

Lately, all the rage is the "side hustle". Many people are exhausted from their main job, and many of these "side hustles" are things that will never replace the income of their job.

Working non-stop trying to "get rich" is sometimes revered as an indication of your level of "badass," ingenuity, or perseverance when really it's just a contest to see who can abandon themselves the most.

Sometimes, I have taken on side work that left me with very little downtime, little relaxation, and feeling constantly grumpy and exhausted.

It's tempting to get caught up in online side hustle solicitations because the seller makes it look easy. ("I started making $10k a month after only three months!") But most of them are too good to be true, take way too much time, and/or require skills you might not have. I honestly believe the side hustle is actually selling the side hustle to others. It's hard to tell if they've ever done it themselves or are simply getting rich selling the "instructions" to others.

Hustle culture is not: having to work three jobs to pay your bills. That's just the shitty side effects of capitalism. Hustle culture is when you think you have to work yourself to death to fit into a society that idolizes "success." It's when you think you're not good enough or your life isn't good enough, so you keep working harder. There is no prize for who works the hardest. In fact, the "prize" is often an ulcer or heart issue.

If you have enough money to live modestly and do the things you love, you do not have to turn every hobby you have into a side hustle. Or turn every spare moment you have into money. Sometimes, you can do things just because you enjoy doing them. Or you can leave... gasp... space in your life for relaxation.

If you're saving up for a specific goal or if you intend to switch careers, then maybe you need to hustle for a bit, but working too many hours for too long is a great way to deplete your immune system and get sick.

Many people see hustling as just another part of the American dream, but it's actually a sign that our culture is toxic and broken.

There's no joy in working yourself to death, not seeing your family, and spending more time at the office than you do at home.

Writer Nicola Jane Hobbs tells us, "We can break the pattern of joyless striving by teaching our nervous system that we can survive the discomfort that arises when we begin to relax and enjoy our lives."[22]

The great news is that you have options and choices! You might not know what they all are right now, but you have them. You just have to look for them.

The best way to avoid hustle culture is to reject the materialism capitalism tries to sell us so you don't have to hustle so much. Not all hustling will get you ahead. Be strategic. Look at how much you'll make and for how many hours of input. Time is a precious asset. Find out how to work less and make more or the same amount.

Ask yourself what your goals are, not just monetary. Figure out how you can get there without hustling yourself to death.

BUILD TANGIBLE SKILLS

Knowledge is a valuable asset in life. Knowing history helps us prevent repeated mistakes. Learning theories, philosophies, and religions help shape our lives and our actions. They help us form ideals and beliefs.

But it's also important to have tangible skills. That's a key to helping us earn a living. Those skills can be things like: teaching, marketing, IT and computer repair, farming, gardening, plumbing, landscaping, and nursing. Basically, anything that can be applied directly to a type of job that is not too obscure.

That's not to say that you shouldn't attempt to follow your dream of being an artist or a philosopher or a poet. But you might find out that it's hard to pay the bills that way (at least at first), and you need to supplement with something else. Yes, having a fallback plan is helpful. We hope we won't need one, but we might. The world can be very uncertain.

Additionally, having practical skills is helpful in the economic shitstorm created by capitalism. Practical skills can help you build community. Growing a vegetable garden helps you access healthy food, get outdoors to enjoy nature, and share with your neighbors. Learning to sew, knit, or crochet allows us to make or mend clothing for ourselves and others. Knowing how to cook is great for gathering people together.

These skills are also things you could market for a small business or cottage industry to make money or make a living under the right circumstances.

CREATE YOUR OWN PATH AND OPPORTUNITIES

I don't know what other kids were told, but here's the path I was led to believe I should follow as a young woman from a rural town: graduate high school, get a job (not a career), find a man, marry that man, have children, work my whole life, and perhaps find some joy after I retire.

However, that path did not appeal to me for many reasons.

First, I did not excel in overly structured work environments, doing work that did not challenge me and working for people who were not invested in my career growth. At all the jobs I worked in my 20s, I became bored quickly because they did not stimulate my creativity or intellect.

Once I moved to a larger city that embraced entrepreneurs and was full of my peers, I was inspired to start a business based on the web development skills I'd been teaching myself, and my life started to flourish in ways I never imagined.

Learning how to build websites was the single best thing I've ever done for myself. Twenty years later, those skills are still how

I support myself and the simple yet rich lifestyle that I enjoy. Web development is the first and only professional skill I've ever had, and I didn't start learning until I was 30 years old. (I mean, it didn't really exist much earlier than that, but still.)

My point is that it's never too late to start. Find something that is marketable (and that you at least somewhat enjoy) and start learning it. You never know where it might lead. If you really want to stand out, learn to do it in a slightly different way than most people do. This will give you an advantage.

I also want to mention that embracing capitalism would've meant I built a bigger web development business, hired people, spent a fortune on marketing, and became the owner/manager of my company instead of the one building websites. Except, I didn't want to be a manager because I enjoy building websites. I enjoy producing creative content (like this book!), and so I again did not do what capitalism expected me to do. Instead, I chose to be happy with my life instead of filling it with high-stress sales and marketing and the challenges that come with the management of other people's labor to make money.

Capitalism wants to put you in a box, but you can break free. You don't have to do things the way others do them. You can make your own path that doesn't turn you into part of the capitalist machine.

MAKE YOUR OWN DEFINITION OF SUCCESS

"The plain fact is that the planet does not need more successful people. But it does desperately need more peacemakers, healers, restorers, storytellers, and lovers of every kind."[23]

David W. Orr

In America, we are taught about the "American dream" from movies, books, magazines, and television commercials. It goes something like this: work until you drop so you can buy a big house, fancy car(s), a pool, luxurious vacations, fancy food at restaurants, the finest cocktails, and name-brand luxury clothing. Sadly, the bank owns your house, and you just rent it from them (with interest) throughout the length of your giant mortgage. You may or may not someday own that house outright. Your car? Also owned by the bank unless you've managed to pay it off.

If your definition of success is "getting rich," how much money do you need to have to be "rich?" Do you just want to feel rich, or do you actually want to be rich?

Chasing money can make people feel like crap. It encourages you to overwork and overspend, creating a vicious cycle of highs and lows and wreaking havoc on your body and mind.

Maybe success isn't about what you own or even how much money you have in the bank. Maybe being rich is about how you feel. What if you measured your success by whether you regularly feel joy and happiness? Perhaps you would change your mind about whether you think you're currently successful (or want to be).

What if success was measured by the amount of downtime you have and the flexibility of your schedule? Would you consider yourself successful right now? What would need to change to achieve that level of success?

Many people think they're going to do all the amazing things in their life when they retire, but so much can happen between now and then. What if you are diagnosed with a serious illness or lose your physical mobility? Will you look back and regret focusing so much on working?

Obviously, we need a certain amount of money to live, but the way we make that money can affect our day-to-day lives. Sometimes, working harder doesn't get us to a better place. Sometimes, it gets us to a much worse place... a place of frustration, physical degradation, and depression. Sometimes, it prevents us from spending time with our loved ones, and we miss the whole journey of life because we're focused on some idea we have about the future.

Capitalism wants us to pursue the traditional American dream, but we can make different choices about how we define success.

FOCUS ON THE DIRECTION YOU WANT TO GO

In life, it is good to have a direction and/or goal. (Or several, but at least one.) Ideally, you will write this goal down on a piece of actual paper using an actual pen. Your goal should align with improving yourself, your life, and/or the world in a tangible way. Your goal might be to run a marathon, replace your super old vehicle, take a trip, make some home improvements, create some art, or move to someplace new.

Having a goal or direction helps guide our actions and priorities. Every day, we can focus on the steps, small or large, we need to take to further our direction or goal. Doing this will bring us joy, satisfaction, and a sense of purpose.

One minute, one hour, and one day at a time, we can make progress. Some days, we'll make no progress! We might even slide backward. But the next day, we can try to make more progress by taking inspired action toward our destination. (While not forgetting to enjoy the adventure along the way.)

One thing capitalism likes to do is distract us from our goals. It puts pretty things in front of us online and tries to get us to spend money that should be for our future and our goals.

If we're not careful, we'll get distracted from how we want to be spending our money, and it can mess up our very important plans.

It's OK to spend time and money on things that are important to you that may not align with your goals. But be sure you're doing it mindfully and not because of impulsiveness, anxiety, or a fear of missing out.

Capitalists want us to act out of emotions, using our hearts instead of our heads. They hire psychologists to learn how to manipulate us with their advertising and sales tactics.

To avoid these targeted ads, we can spend less time on social media and other advertising-intensive internet spaces. Social media itself steals our time and attention, but the advertising is also intended to help us part with our hard-earned money. We have to realize that it's been catered to appeal to each of us individually, which is why the ads seem so enticing to us.

When we find we're getting constantly lost in social media, we can take a step back and reset our usage. We may overuse it if we're stressed and trying to avoid dealing with tough issues or if something distressing is happening in the world. Whatever the reason, learning to be aware of your loss of focus on what's important can help you realign.

Whether your goal is making a shift in your career, engaging in more activism, learning a new skill, moving to a new state, or saving up for that amazing trip, you can get there one step at a time.

FIGHT THE URGE TO COMPETE

If you have to compete too much in your job or business, then you're probably in an oversaturated industry. Dealing with too much competition can feel exhausting and like treading water.

Whether your market is saturated or not, it's helpful to find what differentiates you from other similar employees or businesses and be confident in whatever that thing is.

Are you incredible at customer service? Do you cater to a specific demographic? Use that as your marketing pitch. Find whatever niche you can and be the best at it.

Other businesses or employees, even those who do what you do, can be your collaborators instead of your competitors. You can share knowledge and marketing tactics. You can refer business to each other when your plates are full. You might eventually merge your businesses into one or collaborate on a big project.

Capitalism wants us to compete and be at odds with each other, but we don't have to accept that. We can play nice together and strive for win/win situations because there is plenty of abundance out there for everyone.

Don't participate in the race to the bottom where you and everyone else get the least benefit.

MAKE YOUR BUSINESS CAPITALISM-PROOF

If you're a business owner, you know that not every business will succeed in the long term. As we move to a place where certain resources are more scarce and people are feeling the strain of higher prices, many businesses that aren't very "practical" (like luxury goods or non-essential services) might fall by the wayside or only be accessible to those with much higher incomes. You can monitor the economy to predict when your products or services might need to shift.

Think about what your business offers and how you might make it more practical and accessible. Imagine how you might run your business if your customers suddenly had less disposable income. (You might not have to imagine this.)

How can you make your business more sustainable against economic factors without harming someone else's business? How can you create a win/win for yourself and your customers?

Capitalism can have a negative impact on any industry. It will be helpful for you to examine how it may affect yours.

DON'T COMPARE YOURSELF TO WHERE OTHERS ARE

We are all superheroes just for existing. We all have areas of strength and weakness. If we give the majority of our energy to loving and accepting ourselves, we will see amazing transformations in our lives.

Comparing yourself to where others are in life is a great way to feel terrible about yourself. Here's why: everyone starts off in a different place. You might feel way behind, but you may have started way behind also. You or your family may not have had the resources that others enjoyed. Maybe their parents gave them a business loan, or they had a full ride to college. Stop trying to figure it out. Instead, think about where you used to be compared to where you are now. Think about the progress you've made, the hurdles you've overcome, and the people who've helped you. Focus on where you're going.

Capitalism wants us to compare ourselves to others because "catching up" to people often means spending money. But this life is not a competition. It's a journey that you are on where you try to learn and grow and contribute to the world.

You can go at your own pace without worrying about where you are compared to others. I'm giving you permission to do that.

OWN LESS STUFF TO WORK LESS

The more stuff you own, and the more expensive it is, the more you are tied to making a certain level of earning.

When you own a lot of stuff, even if it's paid for, it still costs money. You have to store it, insure it, maintain it, and otherwise take care of it.

The traditional American dream (sold to us by capitalism) is really an American nightmare that ensures we never have any extra money or time. It goes like this: Make more money, increase the size of your home or apartment, upgrade your vehicle, buy more expensive stuff, rinse, repeat.

The more things you own, the more time and money they will steal from you. Fortunately, there are other ways to use stuff like electrical tools, kayaks, sporting equipment, pickup trucks, boats, jet skis, small kitchen appliances, and lawn equipment without owning it. Use your imagination. You can borrow things from friends. You can rent things. You can find a tool lending library.

Does everyone in the world need a lawn mower that they only use once a week? John Deere probably thinks so, but I don't.

Just because online ads say you need to own something doesn't mean you do. Even if EVERYONE you know owns one. In fact, if that's the case, just borrow it from them. And ask what you can lend them in return.

Don't let your stuff steal your time and joy. Capitalism is lying about what you do and don't need.

RESOURCES

BOOKS:

Big Magic by Elizabeth Gilbert
Ikigai by Héctor García and Francesc Miralles

HOMEWORK:

Make a list of the most expensive things you own. Then, indicate how much it costs to store, maintain, utilize, insure, and fix them. Would you save money if you rented these items only when you needed them? Are any of these items things you no longer use and could donate, consign, or sell?

What one tangible skill could you build that you could share with your community or use to barter?

What are the things that define success for you?

MONEY

INTRO

Money can be a tremendous source of stress in many people's lives. If we have too little of it, we will constantly struggle to get by, build up debt, and suffer the physical effects of economic stress.

Having too much money can also be stressful if making it means you have to work yourself to death, miss out on time with your family, and never get the chance to enjoy life.

Most people need a certain amount of traditional money to survive and thrive, and we can choose what that looks like for us. But any pursuit of money that causes us to compromise our integrity, sacrifice our health, exploit people, or lose sight of the important things in life, probably isn't worth it.

Money is a necessary evil for most people who are alive today. Unless you have managed to fashion a life of self-sufficiency, trade, alternative currencies, and other creative alternatives to money, you probably have to trade your labor in exchange for money you can give to your landlord, insurance companies, and utility providers. (If you're living completely off guavas as currency, kudos to you, and I'd like to learn from you.)

The following are some ways you can try to keep a healthy relationship with money.

KNOW YOUR MONEY PRIORITIES

In a world of 24-hour news, 25,000 television channels, and over a billion websites, the demand for our attention is constant. Social media and other websites are filled with ads enticing us to buy things they've determined are perfect for us. (And, my goodness, they are so right about the things I want!)

The demand for our attention is also a demand for our money, and we only have so much of that. We can't give in to every purchasing whim we have or we will end up living paycheck to paycheck or, worse, severely in debt.

I hear the term "retail therapy" used frequently, and I know shopping is an American "sport," but it will benefit you to break yourself of this expensive mindset. The emotional benefits of shopping are almost always short-lived, often followed by post-purchase regret. Additionally, every time we spend money on something that isn't a priority for us, it takes money away from the things that are.

In her book Financial Feminist, Tori Dunlap advises her readers to pick their three priority spending categories and make sure they're spending... well... prioritizes them.[24]

If you know your goals and priorities, you can consult those when making purchases. Does the purchase fit into your plans and values? Or is it impulsive, unnecessary, or frivolous? Is it good for your mental, physical, and financial health? It's okay to deviate from the plan occasionally, but always ask yourself what you could accomplish instead with the money you're thinking of spending.

I sometimes ask myself how many hours of my life sitting at a desk I am trading for a purchase. As a web developer, I charged $125/hour. So, a pair of expensive yoga pants I recently saw would equal around an hour of my time. Was working an hour at my computer worth a pair of yoga pants? Sometimes it is, especially if they're very high quality, and I know I'll have them for years. This is another reason I only buy high-quality products. Am I going to work at my computer for cheaply made stuff?

I also sometimes take the cost of something I am considering buying and think about what else I could buy with that same money. One expensive pair of yoga pants or a package of 10 yoga classes that I can attend wearing a pair of yoga pants I already own?

These are the kinds of things I weigh to make sure I'm spending my money thoughtfully. If one of the things I'm comparing has no real value to me (booze, something trendy, an article of clothing I love but probably won't wear often), then it will probably lose out to something that will bring me more lasting joy and value.

IMPLEMENT A "NO BUY" JANUARY

The December holidays can be a time when, despite their best efforts, people end up spending more money than they wanted to or anticipated they would.

January is an excellent time to take a pause to evaluate your financial situation after this happens.

It might seem counterintuitive to plan this and then rush to buy some things at the end of December, but spending the minimum amount on groceries and other necessities in January can give you time to assess all your credit card and bank account balances and see where you need to tighten up.

Maybe your version would entail only buying second-hand things and nothing new (thus cutting down on expenses).

The holidays can seem like a consumer marathon (and a capitalistic dream) if we let them. Sometimes, we have the best intentions (like setting a budget for holiday spending) but then end up feeling guilty or inadequate if we don't join in the frenzy.

If you participate in No Buy January, don't think of it as a punishment. Remember that you're doing yourself a favor by re-calibrating your finances so you feel comfortable going forward. Give yourself time to pay down credit card debt before accruing more. Try to avoid those exorbitant capitalist credit card interest fees.

You will find joy in giving yourself some financial breathing room as the year starts.

DON'T BE IN A HURRY

Not only is being in a hurry never fun or joyful, but it also tends to cost us money.

Almost every retail product goes on sale, and if you wait for that, you can often save a ton of money. Paying full price for things is rarely necessary. There are consumable products I regularly buy online that I only buy on sale because I know the company runs regular sales. I try to buy several of each at a time so I can get through to the next coupon code.

Don't waste extra money on priority shipping just to get something quicker that you don't genuinely need quicker. Perhaps you pay monthly for "Prime" to get things delivered more quickly. That's an added monthly expense when almost everything on that large retailer will ship free if you can just wait an extra few days.

You can also, if you're not in a hurry, find many things you need in great condition at thrift shops. From clothes to furniture to kitchen items, thrift shops have so many treasures. You can find your favorite thrift stores near you and check them regularly for the things you need. The same goes for neighborhood tag sales.

Both options keep goods out of landfills and give them new life as your "new" stuff.

Even when you speed on the highway to get somewhere a fraction of a second earlier, you spend extra money (on the extra gas required to do that). You also have a higher risk of getting into an accident, which, as you know, is incredibly spendy (and can permanently damage your body), or getting pulled over by police. By taking the simple step of leaving earlier, you can pay attention, listen to some peppy tunes on the radio, and enjoy the drive instead of spending it in a road rage psychosis.

When you wait until the last minute, you often pay more than full price for things that are in demand. For example, last-minute plane tickets or hotel stays are often inflated because of a lack of supply.

Capitalism counts on people to be in a hurry and make last-minute purchases. While there are occasional last-minute deals, more often, there is a last-minute penalty for those who did not plan accordingly.

SEE THINGS AS THEY ARE

We each have preconceived notions about the world, and when we look around, we often filter what we see and hear based on our existing beliefs about the world.

Sometimes, our filter shows us things as we WISH they were. Capitalism wants us to live in a fantasy world where we have plenty of money to buy a fancy new car, use expensive hair and skin care products, get professional manicures, eat out all the time, and own all the fancy gadgets. They are so good at convincing us that all these things are "normal" that we truly feel "poor" when we try to incorporate them into our lives.

Except we're not poor. We're just living capitalism's dream of making us poor so capitalists can get rich.

We need to be realistic about the kind of life we want. What do the material things add to our life? We may have an idea of what we think they're adding, but are they really adding something, or are we just insecure and think we need these things to be accepted? Do we worry about not fitting in? Where does that worry come from? Why do we care so much about what people think about superficial things?

If you make plenty of money but feel poor, it's time to get real and decide how much of your spending is from the pressures of capitalism. When we spend all our money on material possessions or expensive services, we severely restrict our options in life. There is no time like the present to turn that around. Downsizing your lifestyle can have an unbelievable effect on your quality of life.

DITCH FOMO TO SAVE MONEY

FOMO (fear of missing out) is something folks often include in their social media tags. Despite what your anxious brain might tell you after scrolling through everyone's holiday photos on Instagram, I'm here to tell you that you are not missing out. You are exactly where you're supposed to be doing exactly what you should be doing.

Instagram and Facebook are the kings of FOMO. They're where everyone shows you what restaurants they're eating at, what vacations they're on, and what cool things they just bought. Capitalism loves this! Those photos and videos are free advertising for all the things it's trying to sell you.

If you find yourself in an envious malaise over the fun others have recently had that you didn't, you might start to question why you are not partaking in those things. Does that person make a lot more money than you? How can they afford that? Can you afford that?

FOMO is a form of anxiety caused by grasping for things you don't have. It's a form of attachment that can cause us real pain.

I love traveling, and sometimes, the travel photos people post on social media are almost too much to bear. It makes me want to book a ticket immediately.

But having FOMO can be expensive, and it can lead to very bad and sometimes very expensive decisions.

Do the things and take the trips in the timing that you want to and are able to do the things and take the trips. They will always be out there waiting for you when you're ready. And you might find that some of the things you thought you were missing out on weren't things you wanted to do at all. Take your time without being impulsive.

There's no hurry, and hurrying will make you unhappy one way or another.

VOTE WITH YOUR DOLLARS

Elections only come every few years, but you can still vote for the kind of world you want every single day. Where you choose to buy things can greatly impact the world and your community. I can't overstate this: every time you spend money, you are casting a vote.

When possible, buy from a local independent retailer. I know it costs more, but it supports your neighbors. It also helps ensure that these valuable businesses don't go under. Money spent locally stays local and benefits the whole community.

When you do shop online or at big box retailers (which is sometimes unavoidable), research the companies before you buy. Does one of them give money to oppose issues you care about? Is one of them supporting a terrible candidate or a genocide on the other side of the world?

Maybe find a smaller online retailer. I like to find the original manufacturer of a product I want on Jeff Bezos' retail mega-market online and buy it directly from the manufacturer's website instead. I also order the books on my wish list from my local bookstore using Bookshop.org.

Do I have to wait longer to get my purchases? Sometimes. But is it worth it to give my hard-earned money to businesses that align more with my values? It is to me.

Anytime you support an independent, local business, you are sticking it to capitalism and contributing to a thriving local economy. Defunding bad businesses by spending money more intentionally can bring about lasting change in the world. You can vote every day for the world you want.

SEE THINGS AS INVESTMENTS AND TOOLS

Back in "the day," the world was a much more practical place for many people. Stuff was expensive and not very available.

Not everything you buy needs to be practical, but if you think of your possessions as investments and tools, you might be more apt to choose quality over quantity.

Buy things that will last and that have multiple, practical uses. Buy from reputable businesses, maybe ones with missions you agree with, those who are B Corps, or those who are local. (B Corp Certification demonstrates a company's positive social and environmental impact.)

Purchasing cheap goods with limited lifespans that can't be fixed keeps us in a cycle of shopping and discarding. It's a system created by capitalism that they want us to embrace.

Take care of your belongings so they don't end up in the landfill prematurely. Maintenance and cleaning can extend the life of our belongings, which saves us time and money.

If you've invested in practical tools, you can lend or rent them out to people who don't want to own them. You can barter with neighbors or help people out in emergencies. Remember, you still don't need to own everything because your neighbors will own things, too.

DON'T FALL FOR SUBSCRIPTIONS

One of the best ways for capitalism to make money off you is to get you to sign up for subscriptions. Don't get me wrong; some things are worth subscribing to: your local newspaper's online presence, a monthly donation to a non-profit, or other things you actively and enthusiastically support and use.

Getting you to subscribe to things you probably won't use much (like that New Year's gym membership) is an easy way to get your money.

There's no joy in seeing all the payments you made for something you didn't use. Be sure to keep an eye on your bank and credit card statements so you can cancel unused subscriptions before they cost you too much.

Even subscriptions for practical things like toilet paper or toothpaste can end up costing us more if we don't pay attention to our usage.

Skip the subscriptions whenever possible, even if they appear to save you money. In the long run, they often don't.

BELIEVE IN ABUNDANCE

Despite what marketers might sometimes have you believe, there is plenty of everything for everyone in the world. Yes, some people have greater access to things, but we are only limited by our imagination when trying to find abundance all around us.

Abundance is not just about making money. You can plant a garden and have an abundance of produce during the growing season. You can raise chickens and have an abundance of eggs. You can build community and have an abundance of human resources. The possibilities are endless.

There's so much product waste in the world that could be reused, so much potential that could be maximized, and so many solutions that we could create using all the excess that currently exists in the world.

There are also other sources of abundance, such as time banks and bartering with neighbors for goods or services. (Time banking is a non-monetary system that gives value to our surplus time.) This is where your tangible skills can come in handy.

Where I live, there are fruit trees everywhere, and abundance is the free fruit on the ground in my neighborhood. Most people also share their surplus with friends and neighbors.

Capitalism wants us to believe that abundance is only about making money and buying things, but that is an extremely short-sighted and limited way of viewing the world.

RESOURCES

BOOKS:

Financial Feminism by Tori Dunlap
Growing FREE by Michael Hoag and Laura Oldanie
Your Money or Your Life by Vicki Rubin and Joe Dominguez

WEBSITES:

More about time banks: https://timebanks.org/

HOMEWORK:

What are your money priorities? In what areas can you cut back to have more to spend on your priorities?

What businesses could you STOP spending money with and what businesses could you START spending money with in order to make a positive impact on the world?

CREATIVITY

INTRO

Creativity is how we express ourselves to the world, and it can be liberating and joyful to create for the sheer pleasure of it. In a society that often prioritizes profit over passion, we can reclaim our creative spirit and embrace the art of being creative just because it feels good.

We can celebrate creativity in all its forms, from traditional art to innovative problem-solving, and recognize its power to enrich our lives and defy the capitalist grind.

Creativity isn't just for artists; it's a universal human trait that can manifest in any field, whether it's painting, cooking, or even accounting.

By making room for creativity, you not only enhance your problem-solving skills but also add a sense of adventure and joy to your life. So, let's break free from the idea that everything we do must be productive or profitable and, instead, create for the pure, unadulterated joy of it.

BE CREATIVE JUST BECAUSE

> "*What does the money machine eat? It eats youth, spontaneity, life, beauty and above all it eats creativity. It eats quality and shits out quantity.*"[25]
>
> William S. Burroughs

We all have the ability to be creative at something. Creativity can manifest itself even in unlikely skills like accounting, web development, and even auto repair. Being creative makes you more valuable at your job because, in essence, creativity is related to problem-solving. Creativity can involve finding solutions that aren't obvious, using new materials to create or fix something, or envisioning the design for the catio (cat patio) you want to build. It's so valuable to exercise the creative side of your brain, especially if that's not the part you usually use.

You do not have to be a great artist to be creative. And just because you're not great doesn't mean you're not an artist. You don't actually have to be an artist at all. And frankly, who decides what's great and what's not?

You can create art and engage in creativity because it brings you joy, not because you care what other people think. You don't need to make money with your art to be an artist. If you make art, you are an artist. Being crafty is also creative, so make that cool project you found on YouTube or Pinterest. Or try your hand at painting or pottery.

Being creative and making art is something that feeds the soul and can be meditative. You can make art out of absolutely anything: paint, chalk, markers, garbage, or sand. The sky is the limit, and it doesn't have to be expensive. I particularly like to create paper collage art using old books and postcards I buy at garage sales. Stretch your artsy muscles and enjoy the benefits of losing yourself in the creative process.

DON'T BE AFRAID TO SUCK AT SOMETHING NEW

Playing it safe is an acceptable way to feel content, but sometimes there is joy in trying something new... even if we're not good at it. And honestly, how will you know whether you're good at it until you try it? I mean, have you ever even TRIED wrestling an alligator? (OK, maybe not that.)

Life should be about experimentation and adventure. And failure. There will be lots of failure because most people are not good at every single thing they do, at least not at first. Failure is how we learn. There's very little learning in only doing things you're already great at.

So, pick up that hula hoop. Strap on those rollerblades (and lots of padding). Take that drawing class. Grab a knitting needle. Try some vintage furniture painting methods. Borrow a fishing pole. Rent a stand-up paddleboard. Get out there and do new things!

You should not care what anyone else thinks of your skill level. Everyone has sucked at things. And even if you suck at something, you might love doing it anyway. Nothing should stop you. I'm not an expert at most things I do. I love rollerblading, but I suck real bad at it because I don't practice enough. Do I need to be an expert to enjoy rollerblading? Hell no!

Whatever you do, don't worry about what other people think. You might find joy in trying new, unconventional activities even if you're not great at them.

MAKE EVERY DAY AN ADVENTURE

Even if we're at work (and even if we hate our job), we can add little bits of adventure into each and every day. Life doesn't have to be a constant slog. It should be fun, and we can intentionally make it that way.

We can listen to fun music and dance at our desks. We can sing our way to the bathroom. We can leave inspirational sticky notes around the office (even if we work from home).

We can take a walk at lunch and invite a coworker. We can wear bright and fun clothing or accessories to work. We can bring snacks and share them with the office. We can drive, walk, or bike a different route to work to give ourselves a fresh view.

If we work in an office with coworkers, we can go out of our way to thank them for any assistance they provide us and tell them what a great job they're doing. You'd be amazed at how the vibe in the office can change by one person being upbeat and encouraging.

On the weekends, we can walk around a new neighborhood or drive to a nearby town to explore. We can walk through an alley and notice all the graffiti - some of it might be cool! The more we investigate things closely, the more interesting they become.

Add in talking to strangers to any of these activities, and you've got yourself an exciting time!

We don't have to accept that life has to be ordinary. We can make our own adventure anywhere at any time.

FIND CREATIVE ALTERNATIVES TO "NEW"

Creativity is a way for us to solve problems without involving capitalism. When we don't intend to spend much money (because we don't have it or don't want to), we often find unique solutions to fit something into our budget.

Not everything you buy needs to be new. There are many alternatives to find what we need, many of them better or more unique.

There is an incredible amount of excess stuff in the world, waiting to either find a home or find a dumpster en route to a landfill.

Thrift shops are a great way to find gently used items for a fraction of the cost. There are groups online like Freecycle or other social media groups that exchange goods among their members. You may belong to a time bank that allows the exchange of goods. Tag sales are a fun activity where you never know what you'll find.

If you're adventurous, you can dumpster-dive to see what treasures you can find and remove them from the waste stream.

Despite what societal messages tell us, even gifts do not need to be new and store-bought. Try finding something in great condition at a thrift store. How about a used book that your person loves? What about having an artist make a custom piece of art? Or what if YOU create a custom art or craft item? Something unique that can't be found online.

Thinking outside the box when making purchases can save you a ton of money and result in a much more interesting experience.

EXPLORE ACTIVITIES THAT DON'T COST MONEY

There are an array of hobbies you can pursue even if you're feeling poor or don't want to spend a lot of money. There are things to do with friends that don't force any of you to spend a lot (or any) money. Always remember that some of your friends may not have as much money as you (or you might be the one with less money). You can go for walks at local parks, go for a bike ride, meet at a coffee shop (inexpensive), have a picnic in a park, go kayaking (if you already own kayaks), have a potluck at your house, host board game night, go to a free performance, head to the movies (skip the popcorn and food), volunteer together, and so many other things. We don't always have to meet for a fancy dinner, an expensive event, or pricey cocktails.

The folks in your friend group could take turns choosing or creating a low- or no-cost activity for your next get-together. That way, everyone gets to share in the creativity and add their ideas to the mix.

Anytime you skip the traditional, expensive outings and instead choose a low- or no-cost outing with friends (or alone), capitalism loses, but you win.

FILL YOUR LIFE WITH BEAUTY AND COMFORT

One way to find joy is to fill your surroundings with beautiful things and comfortable furniture. This is especially important to me because I grew up in the 70s and 80s when furniture, carpet, and wallpaper were particularly ugly and depressing. I also grew up in the northeast, where older homes can feel dark and uninspiring. I vowed to always surround myself with pretty things after that experience and to always make sure I could relax in comfort. Doing this is part of the self-care I undertake to counteract capitalism.

Men, this chapter is for you, too, so don't skip it. You deserve to be surrounded by pretty things that inspire you.

Embracing beauty and comfort does not have to be expensive and doesn't have to require giving in to capitalism. If you're patient, you can find everything you need for free or very cheap. You can use plants and thrift store finds to create your perfect oasis. Your friends and neighbors may have plant clippings they will give you, and you can often find free plants online on Craigslist or on community websites or groups. My entire porch is populated with free plants.

Try neighborhood lawn sales for art and pretty things. You should be able to look around your dwelling and always see something that makes you smile.

You should also have furniture that fits your body. Make your surroundings a sanctuary and a place you enjoy being. If you're going to spend money, do it on things that add comfort to your everyday life. You deserve it.

EMBRACE THE EXPERIENCE OF LIFE

Learning to embrace the experience of life with all our senses is a way to get more out of all our days. We can put capitalism out of our heads sometimes so we can enjoy life more.

If we're not fully present, we can go out to dinner, spend a bunch of money, be surrounded by friends, and not have any real memories of the experience afterward. What did we order? How did it taste? What was the texture of the food? What was the conversation about? These are things we can notice and savor.

When you see a bird, you can stop, watch and listen. Where is it going? What does its song sound like? Engage your curiosity.

When you walk outside, feel the breeze. Turn your face to the sun. Feel the sensations on your skin.

Many experiences in life are free, and the best memories are ones we experience with multiple senses and with our full attention.

Capitalism cannot take away our ability to experience life to the fullest extent possible using our senses. We can choose to embrace the experience of life every day.

RESOURCES

BOOKS:

The Creative Act by Rick Rubin
The Book of Ichigo Ichie by Hector Garcia and Francesc Miralles
Nobody Know What They're Doing by Lee Crutchley

HOMEWORK:

The next time you go out to eat, notice everything about the experience. How does the food taste? What is the texture of it? How does it smell? What does the restaurant seating area look like? Is it appealing? What is appealing about it? Is it warm, cold, or somewhere in between? Is there a breeze or a fan or air conditioning blowing on you? What are you having to drink? Can you turn that experience into a lasting memory by focusing on these sensations?

The next time you go somewhere (whether on foot, bike or in your car), take a different route than usual. What new things do you see?

COMMUNITY

INTRO

"One of the most vital ways we sustain ourselves is by building communities of resistance, places where we know we are not alone."[26]

bell hooks

Community is one of our most important assets. In this section, we'll look at the vital importance of human connections and interdependence. In a world that often emphasizes individualism and self-reliance, it's crucial to remember that we thrive through our relationships with others.

We'll delve into practical ways to foster community, from giving back locally and participating in communal activities to the simple yet powerful acts of asking for help and being a cheerleader for others. You'll discover how embracing interdependence can enrich your life and the lives of those around you.

By focusing on collective well-being and mutual support, we can create a more compassionate and resilient society. Get ready to explore the joy and strength that come from being part of a connected, caring community.

FIND YOUR PEOPLE

Whenever I move to a new area, the first thing I do is find my people. Why? First, because having "people" helps me transition more smoothly into my new community. Second, because I know there are other people out there looking for people like me.

So, how do you find your people?

First, start with your immediate neighbors. You have something in common with them because you live in the same area. Do you ever see them out walking or sitting on their porch? Say hello and introduce yourself as their new neighbor. If you're lucky, they're the chatty type, and they'll tell you some things about themselves, like where they're from or what they do for a living. Maybe you'll find some commonalities that endear you to each other. It's great to know your neighbors in times of emergency. You can also get to know your neighbors by joining the NextDoor app or attending neighborhood meetings. Your neighborhood might have a Facebook page. But remember that even if you connect with neighbors online, you will build stronger bonds with people in real life, so invite a few out for coffee or to a neighborhood event.

Second, think of all the things you like to do. Do you love music? Are you a gardener? Do you love to volunteer? An online search can usually find calendars of local events. By going to events that align with your interests, you can meet others who share those interests. There are also often local Facebook groups for certain activities like bicycling, kayaking, music events, and volunteer opportunities.

I know this is more difficult for introverts, but even if you find one group (a book club, a writing group) that can help you connect with like-minded people in your area, it will go a long way toward fostering a sense of community in your life.

I'm a nature lover, so I look for groups like Sierra Club and events like kayaking. I'm also politically active, so I look for organizations to help me get engaged with what's going on locally.

By doing this, I start off in a new place with folks I can lean on in case I need anything. And I can offer to be there for them, which gives me a sense of belonging.

KNOW THAT WE ARE INTERDEPENDENT

"In a real sense all life is inter-related. All men are caught in an inescapable network of mutuality, tied in a single garment of destiny. Whatever affects one directly, affects all indirectly... This is the inter-related structure of reality."[27]

Dr. Martin Luther King, Jr.

While we should strive to take care of ourselves because that is our responsibility, we will always need other people. The world works because we each do our part to provide support for our family, friends, neighbors, and others we encounter.

We would have a tough time accomplishing anything without the people who fill the potholes, the people who take the garbage, the people who ring up our groceries, and the folks who deliver the gas to the gas stations.

When we need something - a recommendation, a shoulder to lean on, a grocery delivery - we usually rely on those in our close circle to help. But every day, strangers do kind things for us that make our lives easier and allow us to function.

No one in this world is an island. Everyone needs other people, often in ways they don't even realize. Capitalism will tell you that some people are "self-made," and that is bullshit. Each successful person needed a thousand things from a thousand people to get where they are (and many started with the advantage of family money).

Back in the hay days when my website business was absolutely killing it, I took thirteen of my best friends to dinner to thank them for the contributions they made to my success. From advice to referrals to shoulders to cry on, I could not have done it without them.

We need each other, whether we admit it or not, so it's best to just admit it. That's the symbiosis of life.

GIVE BACK LOCALLY

In a time where large non-profits are under increasing scrutiny, giving back locally is an excellent opportunity to see how your donation is spent. Even good organizations can succumb to the pressures of greed and capitalism, and it's best to check with a website like Charity Navigator (https://www.charitynavigator.org) to get information if you're looking to donate.

Donating money to a non-profit is not the only way you can help your community.

You can also donate your time as a volunteer or board member. You can donate to online fundraisers for individuals you know who are experiencing accident, sickness, or disease. (Unfortunately, this is currently taking the place of comprehensive healthcare in the U.S.) Donating directly to people lets you have the most insight into where your money is going, and it's also personal to you.

You can donate to local art projects, school fundraisers, your alma mater, or your friend's business crowdfunding campaign. There are so many ways to keep your donation dollars local.

Anything you donate locally makes your neighborhood, town, or city a better place to live for you and everyone else.

ASK FOR HELP

Many of us are terrible at asking for help. We are often first in line to help others but feel that we shouldn't ask for help because we're capable of doing it on our own. Weird, I know! (Capitalism wants us all to feel like "rugged individuals.")

Whether we're capable or not, it's perfectly OK to ask someone to help you lessen your load. In fact, your friends and neighbors WANT to help you, and by never asking them or letting them help you, you're denying them the good feeling of lending a hand. You're also missing out on a bonding experience you could be sharing with them. It's more fun to do things together!

Don't be too proud to ask for help. You're putting yourself at a disadvantage by trying to do everything by yourself. Capitalists hire other people to do many tasks for them. But you have friends, relatives, and neighbors who might love to help out. Plus, if you belong to a local time bank, it's a great place to find willing helpers.

You deserve help and support in life, and you shouldn't be afraid to ask for it.

PARTICIPATE IN YOUR COMMUNITY

Communities work because people participate. In communities where people don't participate, corruption can run rampant, bad people can end up as leaders, and important community issues can be neglected.

In order to be engaged in the health of your community, find at least one committee or association to join in your community. Maybe there's a neighborhood association or an activist group. You can go online and find your closest League of Women Voters, ACLU, NAACP, or other active, civic organizations to join and participate in.

I know capitalism is stretching us all to the breaking point, but one way to fight back is to get involved and not be a bystander. To make sure your views are represented, you have to be at the table. And you can help represent other people who can't be there because of illness, disability, or because they're working parents.

Participating in your community is a great way to meet your neighbors and contribute to positive changes in your area.

HUG EVERYONE

This might seem like a strange inclusion, but hear me out. Everyone needs physical touch and a warm reminder that they're alive. Hugging everyone is a great way to release oxytocin, a type of hormone that promotes positive feelings, in your brain. Hugging can also release brain chemicals that can elevate your mood and reduce your pain – called endorphins.[28] It's not just good for your mind; it's good for your body. But it's not just good for your mind and body. It's also good for society. When you hug people you don't know and don't know anything about, it helps shed the idea that some people are worthy and others aren't. It reinforces our common humanity.

You can use hugging to help you cope with your own emotions. When sadness or anger wells up within you, do something completely unexpected to break the pattern. If you feel angry with someone, give them a big hug instead of engaging in angry rhetoric with them. Draw them away from a divisive exchange.

I understand that not everyone is a stranger-hugging weirdo like myself, so here's an alternative. A "hug" can be any kind gesture as long as it's done without thinking about who the other person is.

When we're going about our daily lives, (I hope) we don't try to analyze what kind of person everyone is just by looking at them. You don't know someone's thoughts, feelings, dreams, or behavior by how they look. We don't decide if we like someone before opening the door for them or letting them merge into traffic in front of us. We assume they're just like us and just going about their day the same as we are.

Why do we assume that? Because that is a correct assumption. Most people are just living their lives, trying to get by, and often struggling just like us. When we do something kind for a stranger, we reaffirm this idea.

Thinking this way is a rebuke to capitalism. Being willing to speak to, hug, or be kind to people we don't know works to end prejudices, assumptions, and divisions between us. Instead of assuming everyone is out to hurt us as the news would have you think, we should assume that everyone is a kind person just like us. That is not to say we should be naive, but if we assume the best about everyone instead of the worst, we may be surprised at how the world changes. Sometimes, we use that filter of expecting the worst in people to bring out the worst in people. So, imagine what would happen if we always expected the best from people.

Maybe the way we act around them would change, and maybe their actions would change, too.

BE A CHEERLEADER

Spreading joy is incredibly rewarding. Taking our joy and multiplying it is as easy as telling someone how great they're doing and that you believe in them.

Take any moment to compliment someone, wish them well, congratulate them, or otherwise share a bit of joy with them... even if you don't feel overly joyful yourself. Sometimes taking the effort to fill someone else with joy can fill you up, too.

Encouragement is something money can't buy and capitalism can't steal. It's free and available to give to everyone.

Be stupidly encouraging. Build people up. Convince them that they really can do all the things they're trying to do. Confidence is often a self fulfilling prophecy. Helping people have more of it can help them go further than they thought they could go.

Be careful not to project your fears of failure on those trying to accomplish incredible things. Even if you can't see how they are going to achieve their goals, be encouraging. Better yet, help them! Offer your assistance. You can see they've created a plan and are going for it no matter what. How can you assist instead of pointing out (or even thinking about) the ways they might fail?

And while you're being a cheerleader for others, be a cheerleader for yourself. Give yourself encouragement and pat yourself on the back for how far you've come and how well you're doing.

PLANT SOMETHING

> *"...make the world a bit better or more beautiful because you have lived in it."*[29]
> Attributed to Pulitzer Prize winner Edward Bok (because patriarchy) but actually said by his grandmother, Welmoet Tideman Bok

If you want to create a lasting impact on the world, plant something.

Plant a tree. Or a hundred. But planting at least one leaf-bearing tree that will grow into maturity will add a precious resource to the Earth.

Plant flowers. Throw some (native) flower seeds into an empty lot or along a barren roadside and watch them grow!

Plant an idea. Share your ideas for peace and justice in the world. Shout them out. Repeat them. Build a movement.

Create art. Putting art out into the world, where it can exist and circulate or be seen for many years is a way to add beauty to the world. Many people can appreciate art over a lifetime, and it can add joy to people's lives.

By doing any of these things, you challenge the notion that only money can add value to the world. You don't need capitalism or financial resources to enhance your surroundings or bring joy to others. Your actions can help others cope with the world a little easier, making a meaningful difference.

TREAD LIGHTLY

Our environment is now impacted by upwards of 8 billion people, each one with the ability to cause damage. We owe it to future generations to think about how our actions affect the world around us and the planet as a whole.

We will never have zero impact on the planet, but we can minimize the damage we do by embracing our role as steward. We can find joy in examining the products and services we use to find the least destructive ones. We can help with cleanup days in our area. We can recycle, find some chickens to feed our compost to, and teach our children the joy of being a protector of animals, nature, and other humans.

Having said that, I want to assure you that there are one hundred companies that cause upwards of 70% or more of the climate change impacts. The four companies with the biggest industrial greenhouse gas emissions (not surprisingly) are ExxonMobile, BP, Shell, and Chevron.[30] Those companies would love for you to believe that climate change is solely your issue to solve.

Having said THAT... here in the United States, our individual impact is far greater than that of people in other countries, which means we could be doing more to lower our own impact.

Along with that, don't throw trash on the ground. Pick up and cut up those plastic 4- and 6-pack holder rings that tend to strangle wildlife. We're not the only ones on the planet. Wild animals are our neighbors. They don't deserve to die because of our trash. Take a walk around your neighborhood once a week and pick up trash. We don't have to live on a planet covered in garbage.

It's a small inconvenience to become aware of how our actions affect our animal neighbors, our human neighbors, and the rest of the planet. Keeping our environment clean and hospitable to wildlife means more joy from nature for us.

RESOURCES

RESOURCES:

The Guerrilla Art Kit by Keri Smith
Zen and the Art of Saving the Planet by Thich Nhat Hanh

HOMEWORK:

What can you do to add beauty and joy to your neighborhood?
What association or board can you join in your neighborhood?

SPIRITUALITY

INTRO

Our spirituality is something that keeps us grounded as we walk through life. In this section, we'll delve into the practices and beliefs that can ground us, bring us peace, and help us navigate the complexities of life.

While we are surrounded by the relentless demands of capitalism, it's crucial to find ways to connect with our inner selves and the broader universe. This section explores various spiritual practices that foster compassion, joy, and a sense of interconnectedness.

By embracing spiritual practices, you can counteract the stress and fragmentation of modern life, fostering a deeper connection with yourself and others. Let's explore how these spiritual tools can help you lead a more balanced, joyful, and meaningful life.

WISH FOR THE BEST FOR YOURSELF AND OTHERS

Reciting the loving-kindness prayer/meditation can help you build compassion for yourself and others. Below is my version of the loving-kindness meditation:

May I be safe and protected
May I be healthy in body and mind
May I feel joy and love and happiness
May I live with ease

Next, I insert the name of someone I'm in conflict with and repeat the phrases. This helps me when I am feeling frustrated with someone. It reminds me that I am upset with the behavior, not the person, and that I don't want that person to suffer. It also helps relieve my own suffering about whatever incident(s) caused my frustration. We should never turn one act of meanness or violence into another one. Many people today are vengeful, and this is a very dangerous mindset to have.

May _____ be safe and protected
May _____ be healthy in mind and body
May _____ feel joy and love and happiness
May _____ live with ease

I am very sincere when I recite these words. I picture the person in my head and how their pain may have caused them to behave in a way that hurt or upset me. Then, I wish for their causes of pain to be gone so they can be happy.

Then, I usually think of a loved one who is struggling, and I wish them peace and loving-kindness.

May _____ be safe and protected
May _____ be healthy in mind and body
May _____ feel joy and love and happiness
May _____ live with ease

Lastly, I wish for everyone, no matter who or where, to have safety, health, happiness, and a life free of suffering.

May we all be safe and protected
May we all be healthy in body and mind
May we all feel joy and love and happiness
May we all live with ease

This is a nice way to end your day before falling asleep. It fills you with positive feelings toward yourself and others. It reminds us that we're all human, and we all want to be safe, healthy, joyful, and to have a life without struggle.

PRIORITIZE JOY

Everywhere in the world, no matter where you are or what your circumstance, there is joy around you. When you become good at being present and noticing, you will understand this.

Some people may feel that they don't "deserve" joy. Perhaps you were taught that this life is about suffering, and all your reward will come in the next one. Respectfully, that is bullshit. No god would put us on this Earth simply to toil and be miserable. Any god that created such beauty would want us to enjoy it.

Because we spend so much time under stress - financial, emotional, mental, and physical – we might feel that there is no joy available to us. But joy will not always come to us, so we have to make time to go to it. We have to prioritize time in joyful situations and surroundings, and they are everywhere.

Maybe there's a park nearby or a botanical garden. Maybe a neighborhood with some murals or lovely landscaping. It's optimal if you can find joy in a place you can walk to. Driving is not always joyful, so it's nice to be able to walk out your door and have a joyful destination. (But if you have to drive, that's OK, too.)

Maybe you just need to pay more attention to your pet. They are a tremendous source of joy if you let them be. Maybe you love dancing and haven't been in a while. What are the things that make your heart sing?

Joy is all the little things that we often don't notice or give priority to because of life's stressors. Joy is a rose that you spend a full 30 seconds smelling and appreciating. Joy is the feeling of gratitude that your neighborhood has a park with trees and flowers. Joy is saying hello to someone on the street and asking if you can pet their dog. Joy is a feeling of slowness. It's a space of time during which you can truly notice any and all of the little nuances about your surroundings.

There is nature everywhere. You simply have to notice it or find it. There are insects, animals, and plants either thriving or fighting for the biological imperative of survival. There are sunsets and sunrises that can be seen from anywhere in the world.

Find a few things that consistently bring you joy and keep them in your toolbox when you need them. It's best to prioritize joy before you need it, though. Make it a regular habit.

Don't let corporate ads convince you that you'll only find joy in purchases and possessions. Marketers are paid to make you think that, but you can think for yourself.

The more you can find joy in things that don't cost money (like nature), the more you'll be sticking it to capitalism. Corporations want you to find joy in their expensive products, but you don't need any of those things to feel joy. In fact, the expense of those things might have the opposite effect.

BELIEVE IN SOMETHING

"Heaven is my father and Earth is my mother... All people are my brothers and sisters, and all things are my companions."[31]
                      Confucius (the father of Confucianism)

Our religious or spiritual beliefs are often learned through our families while we're very young. If this is the case, it's beneficial to examine these beliefs as an adult to see if they're still consistent with our values. Many people who grew up in oppressive religions like Catholicism, Pentecostal, or other evangelical religions come to see that these religions are a bastardization of the loving teachings of Jesus in the only testament that should matter to a Christian: the New Testament.

    The main premise of a religion or spiritual belief should be to help us become good people, not to punish ourselves or others. Three of the largest religions (Christianity, Islam, and Judaism) all worship the same god, but you wouldn't know that if you talked to some of the people who practice them. When practiced correctly, religion should be used to gain strength, get through hardships and challenges, and grow as a person.

Some of us don't follow a religion but have strong beliefs about nature and kindness and making the world a better place. We may create our own spiritual beliefs and practices that guide our lives and help us weather life's ups and downs.

There are many other religions and philosophies in the world for gathering guidance and strength. A few of the more interesting ones are Sikhism, Confucianism, Buddhism, Taoism, Baha'i, Zoroastrianism, and Hinduism. There is absolutely nothing wrong with pulling out the best parts of any of these to form your belief system.

While Buddhism, Taoism, and Confucianism aren't religions, they are philosophies that can help guide our lives. They can teach us how to treat ourselves, other people, and the Earth.

I wrote my own manifesto to remind myself of what my values and beliefs are so I can get back on track if I'm not acting the way I should. Here are some things I believe in:

- Gratitude

- Respecting the Earth

- The idea that most people are good

- Treating life with reverence

- Living authentically

You should have a set of beliefs designed to make you a better person and guide your everyday behavior.

SPEND TIME IN NATURE

> "If you truly love nature, you will find beauty everywhere."[32]
>
> Vincent van Gogh

Spending time in nature is known to reduce stress and help us focus.

Being where it's quiet, without the distraction of our work or home life, can be so valuable. Natural places are where we can turn off our phones and be present.

Nature is the place where focusing our attention on what's around us can provide joy to our senses. Birds chirping, squirrels rustling, fresh air, the texture of the trees, the trail under our feet – these are all things we can notice and savor.

Being in nature reminds us that life can be simple and doesn't need to be filled with the clutter of materialism and technology.

There are many places in nature that we can go to for free. There are also places like national parks we have to pay to enter, but whose entry fee helps protect those places from the greed of capitalism. To capitalists, an undeveloped piece of land is a set of natural resources yet to be exploited by them.

Our survival as a species and the enjoyment of our time on this planet are both tied to the health of the natural world, so visiting more natural places and experiencing the joy we get from them will help motivate us to protect them.

HAVE RITUALS

Our daily habits help dictate how our lives will unfold. Rituals are similar but are often more spiritual in nature. Meditation could be considered a habit but is also a spiritual ritual.

Having rituals that ground us in our spirituality and love of life and the planet can guide us in our anti-capitalism endeavors.

Your morning ritual may be to do yoga, meditate, and then read some affirmations that will help guide your day in a positive direction. You may have tea in your garden or say prayers. I read my personal manifesto every morning to affirm my commitment to being the kind of person I'm proud to be.

Our rituals can be a way we affirm our dedication to love, joy, and truth. They can honor those who came before us and be a promise to those who come after. My ancestors, for example, were farmers. They cared for and tended hundreds of acres of land in my hometown. They loved the Earth and depended on it to provide for them and my family. I want to steward the Earth inasmuch as I can for my nieces, nephews, grand-nieces, grand-nephews, and all the future descendants in my family.

RADIATE PEACE

Thich Nhat Hanh said, "If we want peace, we have to be peace. Peace is a practice and not a hope."[33]

Peace begins with each one of us. It starts with finding peace within ourselves. Once we find peace and contentment in our own lives, we can cultivate a peaceful heart that no one's words or actions can penetrate.

We can learn to respond to the world without violence or revenge. We can learn to be thoughtful in our interactions with people and not perpetuate the senseless nastiness of social media or other public interactions.

If we're peaceful people, nothing anyone does or says should change that. That's who we are regardless of outside influence. We can choose to be an example of peace that others can follow.

Capitalism thrives on chaos and violence. We can choose not to feed it and choose peace instead.

GIVE PEOPLE GRACE

When we have cultivated a peaceful heart, we can more easily give people grace. Giving people grace means not being hard on them when they make an honest mistake. Giving people grace is about knowing that none of us are perfect. We all make mistakes, and it's not beneficial or kind to hold people to unreasonable standards concerning those mistakes.

Giving other people grace is easier if we first learn to give it to ourselves. Many of us hold ourselves to unreasonable standards (like working too much, giving too much, being perfectionists, and punishing ourselves for every little mistake). If we think that's what we should be doing, we will probably think that's what others should be doing.

We never know what others are going through, so we don't need to punish them for every perceived slight when interacting with them. Obviously, we want to be treated with respect, but often, we can choose not to focus on a single interaction with someone or even many. We can choose not to take things personally.

Some people have just lost a loved one. Many are struggling to survive financially in our cruel system of capitalism. Others are struggling with physical or mental health issues. Most of the time, we really don't know. So, if the barista is short with you, you don't need to dwell on it. Service workers have thankless jobs. Maybe go out of your way to make the person feel appreciated instead of taking it personally. That's what grace is.

RESOURCES

BOOKS:

The Art of Living: Peace and Freedom in the Here and Now by Thich Nhat Hanh
The Little Book of Inner Peace by Ashley Davis Bush
You Need a Manifesto by Charlotte Burgess-Auburn
Siddhartha by Hermann Hesse

HOMEWORK:

When you wake up in the morning, think of three things you are grateful for. If you like, write them down in a gratitude journal so you can look back on them later.

Repeat the loving-kindness meditation each night and include a person or group of people that you don't like or are in conflict with.

Try to be more aware of when you are focusing on a negative interaction with a stranger. Imagine they are a friend of yours who's going through a rough time. Let go of your attachment to feeling negatively toward them.

CIVICS

INTRO

Civics is about how we conduct ourselves as members of our local, state, national, and global communities. In this section, we'll explore how to be an engaged, compassionate, and active citizen in a world that often encourages apathy and division.

This section encourages you to extend kindness beyond your immediate circle and engage in meaningful ways with your community. Whether it's through voting, joining movements, or simply giving a damn about important issues, your actions can make a significant difference.

By focusing on unity, informed activism, and peaceful engagement, we can collectively challenge the status quo and work towards a society where everyone has a fair shot. Let's dive into how you can play a crucial role in shaping a better future through conscious civic participation.

BE KIND

This may seem obvious, but you should be kind. Beyond your immediate circle. Beyond your community. Beyond people you know. Just be kind to everyone, regardless of the circumstances.

And don't ever condition being kind to someone based on who they are or whether you like them. Be kind for the sake of kindness. Be kind because you are a kind person.

One thing capitalism doesn't want everyone to do is get along. It very much wants us to be in conflict with each other. Therefore, being kind is a radical act of defiance against the divisive forces of capitalism.

As a general rule, happy, kind people don't need material things to fill a hole in their lives caused by anger and conflict. For this reason, capitalism wants to keep us divided and fighting so we'll keep buying and spending. But you don't have to succumb to that imperative.

A whole lot of unkind sentiment is expressed on social media. Facebook's algorithm is programmed to show us things that will play on our negative emotions. And then, we make the mistake of reading the comments.

We see people saying uninformed or downright cruel things. And we think to ourselves, "I am smarter than this person. I can inform them. And I also might be a bit of a snarky twat about it." But there's an alternative.

You can say nothing.

Or, if you really must say something, you can find something positive to say that will inspire people who are reading the comments instead of adding to their anger, sadness, or frustration.

I shouldn't have to say this, but never wish harm on anyone... in your mind, online, in-person... just never. It puts terribly juju out into the Universe.

Even if the issue is really serious and really important, we don't have to add to the outrage. People need hope, too. How can you add to the conversation without simply intensifying it? Without simply inflaming it? Without having to use caustic humor? You can be an agent of change who changes the narrative.

How can your comment make other people in the comments see that they have an ally in you who has hope for a positive resolution? Can you suggest they take concrete action that might help alleviate the situation? How can your comment be constructive?

And what example can they take from how you speak? What example can the uninformed person take from how you speak? What ideas are you representing, and how can you make those ideas attractive to others? Probably not by being an absolute toad about it.

How can you get the person you disagree with to agree with you on something? That's how we find our common humanity, and you'd be surprised at how many people agree that capitalism sucks donkey balls.

If we post unkind things about strangers and "others" on social media, we're perpetuating capitalism's plan to divide us. Divided, we're weaker. (That's why unions are making a comeback.) Whenever I see that someone has purchased a "So-and-so Sucks" t-shirt, I see capitalism at work. People will jump on any message that appeals to people's perceived outrage.

That's not to say you can't disagree with people. But refrain from name-calling. If you're name-calling, then you're probably too emotional to be in the conversation. Wait until you can use neutral language to express your point. You will help de-escalate the rhetoric in this way, which benefits everyone.

You don't need to make other people's lives more unhappy or more difficult. Everyone is already dealing with their own personal battles. Treat others nicer than they treat you. Flip the narrative. Be surprising. Sometimes, when I see someone post something incredibly heartless on social media, I respond with, "You could really use a hug, my friend." And while they may take this as snark, I am being 100% serious (because I am the "quirky hug lady" who goes to events and hugs strangers). Sometimes, they question if I would actually give them a hug, and I tell them that everyone who wants hugs from me gets hugs from me.

Happy people aren't generally mean. Often, people who are hurting the most are the ones online who throw insults. Remind yourself how grateful you are that you're not as miserable as that person. And if that person is already in pain, you do not need to add to it by being a sarcastic tool. Let them rant until they're blue in the face, but you don't need to contribute. If you are the miserable one, please stay off social media with your garbage comments until you're feeling more at ease.

Being unkind is contagious. It's like the butterfly effect. When someone is angry with you, then you get angry at someone around you. Then that person gets angry with someone they know. And the cycle goes on and may escalate until someone breaks it. You can break it. You can choose to do that.

You can create the butterfly effect of kindness instead.

GIVE A SHIT ABOUT SOMETHING

Capitalists want us to focus on ourselves and our needs and how they can help us fulfill those needs with their products and services. But the world does not, in fact, revolve around us, and there are big issues that need our help.

Think about what issues are important to you and give a shit about them. Giving a shit means doing something about them. Talk about them, donate money to them, volunteer your time, and contact your elected officials about them. Maybe even protest about them!

Things get done in this country because ordinary people like you and I give a shit about them and show up for the people affected by them - especially local issues that might not have a prominent, national non-profit to assist them.

Whether your issue is the treatment of animals, the environment, women's rights, LGBT rights, homelessness or housing, your contribution can make a big difference. And don't forget about the essential ingredients of life: clean air, water, soil, housing, education, and food. These are all things we need to continually fight to keep out of corporate hands so everyone will have access to them.

We have workplace protections, women have the right to vote, and Black Americans have some semblance of equality because ordinary people demanded it. Those things didn't happen because of the generosity of corporations or the government. They were made possible by groups of people who gave a shit and dared to fight for what was right.

EXERCISE YOUR DUTY TO VOTE

Unlike members of the capitalist ruling class in both major political parties, I'm not going to tell you to vote for one of the presidential candidates they hand-picked for you. (Because really, they did pick them, even if you have the illusion that you did.)

I'm not going to tell you that you have to vote for anyone for president if you think both candidates are absolutely horrible for America (and they increasingly are). We also have some "third-party" candidates who could do great things for this country if given the chance. They could also suck. We really don't know because it's been impossible to get one of them elected.

But you should always, always, always vote for all the other down-ballot candidates because they are often as or more important than who gets elected President of the United States.

The people who get elected to your local city or town council have an inordinate amount of control over your daily life. The school board controls what your children learn. The police chief determines how/when to enforce local laws. Your state legislators control a lot of your life with the laws they make and how they direct them to be enforced.

I know it's time-consuming, but try to research the candidates on the ballot. Do they receive donations (and thus provide influence) from entities that damage our democracy (like foreign influence, fossil fuel companies, weapons manufacturers, and military contractors)? Organizations like the League of Women Voters can provide information on candidates. Do your homework as a citizen so we can create the kind of country that works for the majority of us.

It's vitally important to vote, but remember that it is only part of your civic duties.

JOIN A MOVEMENT

My advice: choose what issue is most important to you and join a large-scale movement that disrupts those who control it. That will often have a more lasting impact than who you vote for to sit in the Oval Office.

Non-violent civil disobedience is, in part, how we got women's rights, civil rights, and a whole bunch of other rights. When a large group of concerned citizens shows up and blocks roads, bridges, streets, and commerce, elected officials listen. They also try to stop you from doing that, so pay attention to legislation that impacts your First Amendment right to peaceably gather. And remember: if it weren't effective, they wouldn't try to prohibit it.

When you join a movement for liberation anywhere in the world, you indirectly help yourself. Any powerful military force that tries to oppress a people gives confidence to other powerful military forces to oppress other people. And, at some point, it might be you they're trying to oppress. The war machine is an arm of capitalism. Just be sure you know who the real oppressor is in any given scenario because sometimes the oppressor plays the victim. (P.S. It's the one with the heaviest artillery.)

Peaceful movements are historically the most effective. When I've participated in civil disobedience, the message is clear: do not be "that person" (who resists or tries to cause chaos). Mass (peaceful) arrests are great PR for civic movements. Know that the police may not always be on board with your peacefulness, but the price for progress is mass protests that shut down business as usual and are impossible for capitalists to ignore.

LEARN ABOUT COLONIALISM AND PATRIARCHY

If you're a guy, don't get your knickers in a wad about the term "patriarchy." It's an integral part of the history of the world that you should know about. Being part of the patriarchy means you are perpetuating the patriarchy, and the only way to avoid that is to know more about what it means.

Patriarchy is a system whereby men (mostly those considered white) have the most power and fight to keep that power. The way they historically do that is by preventing women or "non-white" people from having rights – such as the right to vote, the right to own property, the right to use banks, etc. Women, for instance, could not open a credit card without their husband's signature until 1974.

Women and Black Americans fought to get equal (kind of) rights in the U.S., and since then, they have naturally become more successful. With equal footing as white men (kind of), more women now go to college than men, and Black men and women (some of whose ancestors originally entered this country as slave labor to make southerner capitalists wealthy) have become successful athletes, actors, musicians, academics, and businesspeople.

This makes the patriarchy feel very insecure. After a period of women and people of color becoming successful (in a system where men historically have not had to work as hard to be more successful than everyone else), men are suddenly having to play catch-up to protect their positions of power.

Again, if you're a white guy, this is your opportunity to learn and do better. If you're reading this and you think women and people of color want special rights, you're wrong (and you know that). They just want the same rights and opportunities as you, but many people continue to deny them those rights out of insecurity. Did you know some states have closed a bunch of voting locations in predominantly Black neighborhoods? Did you know we're the only developed country without paid maternity leave? These are disadvantages created by the patriarchy.

If the only way white men can feel good about themselves is by sabotaging other people's success... well, that's just sad. Don't be sad. Be secure about yourself and your place in this world. You have value. There is joy in paying attention to your own damn life. But yeah, if you're a guy who's been skating by on your very own identity politics, then you might have to put in some extra effort... or, as women call it, the normal amount of effort that we usually put into everything just to be considered equal to men. (Also, we do it while bleeding, creating and carrying human life, and going through heinous hormonal changes in our 40s.)

The patriarchy doesn't want social progress in the world because social progress looks like them ceding some of their power to others. This thought scares them because they are selfish chuckleheads. Don't be a selfish chucklehead. Other people don't have to fail for you to succeed. Women understand this because they are more collaborative. We generally want everyone to win.

Colonialism is another byproduct of the patriarchy. It's where (almost exclusively) men fulfill their fantasies of conquest in the form of one country (the colonizer) invading another country (usually a poor one with black or brown residents) to make money off whatever valuable resources are there. Colonialism happens when the invading country kills as many of the poor country's residents as is needed to steal the resource they want to steal. Often, the colonizer sets up a system to keep siphoning those resources for an extended period of time.

In settler colonialism, the colonizer wants to steal the land of the poor country. That generally involves killing many more of the current residents who undoubtedly will not want to hand over their homeland to a bunch of invading thugs. It also might involve the enslavement of the native populations. Colonialism is about money and capitalism. It's about exploiting stolen resources, labor, and land.

Knowing about patriarchy and colonialism can help you see and understand the damage capitalism has done (and continues to do) to the U.S. and the world.

RAGE AGAINST THE MACHINE

It's important to know whose side you're on. Be able to recognize the people and entities in power and with the money and resources. This is a class war against the ruling/monied class. It's not a culture war, as capitalists would like you to believe. Direct your anger and outrage toward a) fighting the system of oppression and b) helping those affected by it.

Look to the disadvantaged communities around you. Look at the marginalized people. Look to the women and people of color. Who is trying to control and exploit them? Those are the people to fight against because they will screw you, too.

Don't let propaganda make you believe that the powerful people are the victims. Most media is owned by capitalists, too. Read books. Search out information from independent, reliable sources.

You should know that the police are part of the "machine." Yes, there may be individual policemen and women who are good, but the police do not work for you. The police, almost without exception, work for capitalism. Capitalists engage the police to protect their physical assets. Police shouldn't need riot gear and military equipment to deal with ordinary American citizens. That's how you know they're not working for us. When we protest en masse, we threaten capitalism's power. Remember this, as we will need to protest more to get us out of this late-stage capitalist mess we're in. The police may become increasingly violent as the ruling class feels their power is threatened.

There is joy and pride in standing up for communities fighting for liberty, autonomy, and freedom. In the end, we're all in this together because any of us could end up on the wrong end of a police encounter and/or the poverty line at any time.

This is why it's so important that we stick together and join forces against capitalism.

BUT DON'T FALL FOR OUTRAGE BAIT

Media outlets often choose headlines intended to cause lots of "dialogue" in the comments, and people say a lot of dumb things in response. However, we can refuse to become outraged at other average people because of media or social media. We can refuse to participate in the outrage machine that aims to divide us against each other and make us forget about who causes the real problems in this world (capitalism, greed, corporations, corrupt politicians).

It's not the single mother on food stamps or the asylum seeker fleeing violence (from a country we probably destabilized) that is causing problems in your life. It's also not the MAGA follower who is struggling financially and wondering why neither side wants to help him. They're just as unhappy as you are.

Stop wasting so much energy blaming the wrong people for your unhappiness. In comedy, they say not to punch down or make fun of people who are less powerful or privileged than you. It's a bad look. That's what I'm telling you: don't punch down or even sideways. Those people have no more influence on the world than you do. Punch up. Always punch up to the ruling class and influential people. They make and enforce the rules.

We can be better than capitalists want us to be. We can defy their divide-and-conquer strategy and refuse to give clicks to clickbaiters.

I assure you that there is nothing other average Americans can do that would ever equal what corporate America and globalism steal from us. First, the media tends to highlight something an infinitesimal number of people are doing and make it a big deal. Are 0.001% of welfare recipients lying to get it? Who gives a fuck. Corporations get government welfare AND hide their money in other countries AND avoid taxes using the loophole laws they lobbied Congress to pass, all while making record profits off you. Did your conservative neighbor work under the table to avoid taxes? Great! We should all do that. Even if we ALL did that, it still wouldn't make up for the corporate abuses we all already pay for. All that energy you're using to care so much about these teeny, inconsequential things could be used to focus on the real, actual problem, which is the way capitalists keep us distracted from their attempts to control our lives and everything we do. Capitalism doesn't have a soul or empathy. They love it when you blame the red ones or the blue ones, the poor ones or the "foreigners."

When we have the courage to look past the easy scapegoats and see the big picture of who causes problems in our country, we can start making real change. Until then, don't take the bait.

DON'T GET DISTRACTED

Keep your eyes on the prize: a society where we take care of each other and treat everyone with equal respect and dignity. When you interact in person or online, remember that these are our shared goals. Ask yourself if your current contribution to the narrative is getting us closer to these goals.

Don't get caught up in lateral fighting. Always punch upwards toward the ruling class.

The best way to fix our economic and political systems is to keep more wealth in the bottom 99% and get money out of our political system. Excessive corporate political contributions have no place in a democratic country. Every citizen should have the same power to influence our candidates and leaders. Corporations are, in fact, NOT people. They are a collection of organizing documents that we should treat as revocable (and that are revocable, even though we rarely exercise that power, even in the most egregious of cases).

You can help fix this by voting for candidates up and down the ballot who are committed to reducing the influence of corporate money on politics. But be careful to look at their actions and not just their words.

Aside from that, join coalitions of people, groups, and organizations working toward this goal. You might get more done that way than counting on an elected official, with his/her own agenda, to do the work for you.

PARTICIPATE

You don't get a trophy for civic participation, but you do get closer to a functioning democracy, and that's pretty cool.

You should go to your neighborhood association meetings if you have one. Go to your city council meetings. Answer surveys from your city or town. You can't be represented if you're not present. You may find that there are loads of issues that you usually never even hear about until it's too late.

If a new development is proposed near you that would be terrible, get involved. You have power as a citizen, and you should use it. Even better, bring five friends with you. Now you've increased your power times five. See how that works? Wear matching t-shirts. Now you're visible.

When you participate, you will also see how the powerful opposition tries to squash your influence. Remember that if they're doing it to you, they're doing it to others. It will help you understand how the system works. Your fight is everyone's fight. Everyone's fight is your fight. We're all trying to prevent big businesses from ruining or gentrifying our city, town, or neighborhood and driving out small businesses and longtime residents who can't afford the new reality that's being created. And that's just one of many local issues you might be compelled to engage with.

Capitalism counts on keeping you busy, tired, and distracted so you won't participate, but we need good people taking the time to show up and participate.

TRAVEL

This one might feel like a luxury, but travel is incredibly beneficial, whether it's to another town, another state, or another country.

Getting out of our bubble helps us learn about how others experience the world. It exposes us to other cultures, even those in other US cities and states.

When you travel, you can start conversations with the locals, eat the kind of food they eat (no golden arches!), listen to the music they listen to, and engage in whatever cultural experiences they have.

Use public transportation at home and abroad. Mingle with people you normally wouldn't encounter. Capitalism likes to keep us separated so we believe the scary or insulting tropes about others.

It's less easy to stereotype and judge people once you meet and learn about them. They become real to you. Human even.

Travel doesn't have to be expensive, and there are many creative ways to do it cheaply.

Even a little travel goes a long way.

BE A PEACEMAKER

The world is full of violence and anger, so what we really need are more people dedicated to peace and justice. The kind of peace I'm talking about is diplomacy and levelheadedness. It is possible to get "peace" through force by oppressing people, but that's not real peace.

Peace is when everyone is allowed to enjoy their life and have equal access to rights and resources.

Capitalism contributes to an enormous amount of violence in the world. It protects itself brutally and uses brutality to extract resources from communities that don't want to give up those resources - resources like development land, fossil fuels, agricultural land, water, and other valuable cornerstones of life. The military-industrial complex is just a collection of large corporations that profit from war - manufacturers of weapons and surveillance equipment, mercenary contractors, and anyone involved in the construction or cleanup from a war. The military-industrial complex does not want peace because they do not benefit from it.

They can only serve their shareholders when there's bloodshed and destruction.

You can be a peacemaker by not supporting the war machine with your money (purchases, investments, etc). You can also protest wars and cause headaches for the companies that contribute to or profit from them. And you can be peaceful in your interactions with other people. Violent language and rhetoric contribute to the violent atmosphere in the world.

Think peaceful thoughts, speak peaceful words, and engage in peaceful actions to contribute to a more peaceful world.

RESOURCES

BOOKS:

It's OK to be Angry About Capitalism by Bernie Sanders
I'm Right and You're an Idiot by James Hoggan

EXERCISE:

When you're on social media, challenge yourself to leave only helpful, positive, and encouraging comments. Use the "love" reaction copiously. If you see something you disagree with and simply must respond, be kind, constructive, and thoughtful. Social media is not an emotional dumping ground where you have permission to shit on everyone's day. Being intentionally kind in the comments and being encouraging in your responses to posts will actually put you in a better mood and improve your own day. Try to see social media as a place where you can do a public service by helping to elevate joy for yourself and others.

THE STUFF AT THE END

CONCLUSION

Am I suggesting we get rid of all capitalism entirely? Not at all. What I'd like to suggest is that we stop allowing wealth hoarding by big corporations and billionaires and the resulting impoverishment of the middle class. The middle class was the strongest in the U.S. when we judiciously taxed excessive income and wealth and used that revenue to make America stronger. But we'll have to fight with all our power to force our current ruling class to do what's right.

With that in mind, here's the big takeaway:

Reject the notion that joy must come with a price tag and understand that true happiness can be found in the simple aspects of life. Capitalism might try to sell you on the idea that your worth is measured by your possessions and bank balance, but you can redefine success.

By focusing on what truly matters—your mental and physical well-being, creativity, and connections with others—you can resist the capitalist urge to compete endlessly and instead collaborate and build a supportive community. Embrace your individuality, create your own path, and redefine what it means to be successful. Remember, it's not about how much you have but about how much joy you can cultivate and share. So, go ahead, plant a tree, create art, and build relationships. In doing so, you'll leave the world a bit better and a lot more beautiful than you found it.

Lastly, always punch up because the real fight isn't against each other; it's against the system that tries to keep us divided and distracted while it robs us of money, liberty, and dignity. This is and always has been a class war.

MANIFESTO OF JOY

1. We will have more joy if we take care of our human bodies

2. We can seek contentedness in our lives by ending our unhealthy attachment to material things

3. We can seek joy within and around ourselves at any time

4. We can help bring joy to others through our kindness

5. We can be committed to helping remove barriers to joy

6. We can reject incitements to feel fear of others

7. We are empowered to stand up to arbiters of fear

8. We can see other ordinary folks as allies, not opponents

9. We can fight for a future of joy where people's basic needs and well-being are placed above profits

SHOUT-OUTS

I want to start off by acknowledging my cat, Libby, whose unconditional love and affection get me through even the worst days.

Then, I'd like to thank my beta readers for providing invaluable feedback on the content of this book. I'd also like to thank all my family, friends, and encouragers. I have truly managed to surround myself with amazing humans.

Also, I'd like to acknowledge Valerie Kaur (whose book *See No Stranger* I read while writing this one), who embodies the idea that we can stay kind and loving even when bad things are happening around us.

Lastly, a shout-out to Ijeoma Oluo, an incredible author and human whose writing and social media presence are so incredibly thoughtful and insightful. They inspire me every day to keep fighting this fight.

CITATIONS

1. brown, adrienne maree. "The Power in Pleasure." YES! Magazine, 18 May 2022, www.yesmagazine.org/issue/pleasure/2022/05/18/power-in-pleasure-adrienne-maree-brown. Accessed 25 June 2024.

2. American Cancer Society. "Key Statistics for Mesothelioma." *American Cancer Society*, 8 Aug. 2023, www.cancer.org/cancer/types/malignant-mesothelioma/about/key-statistics.html. Accessed 25 June 2024.

3. Gabler, Ellen. "EPA Bans Asbestos, a Deadly Carcinogen Still in Use Decades After a Partial Ban Was Enacted." *NBC New York*, 5 Apr. 2023, www.nbcnewyork.com/news/national-international/epa-bans-asbestos-a-deadly-carcinogen-still-in-use-decades-after-a-partial-ban-was-enacted/5235832/. Accessed 25 June 2024.

4. Pope Francis. Laudato Si': On Care for Our Common Home. Encyclical Letter, Vatican Press, 2015.

5. Chödrön, Pema. *Living Beautifully: with Uncertainty and Change.* Shambhala Publications, 2012, p. 60.

6. Goldsmith, Marshall. *Triggers: Creating Behavior That Lasts--Becoming the Person You Want to Be.* Crown Business, 2015, p. 54.

7. Kornfield, Jack. *The Art of Forgiveness, Lovingkindness, and Peace.* Bantam Books, 2002, p. 67.

8. Nowak, Anita. *Purposeful Empathy: Tapping Our Hidden Superpower for Personal, Organizational, and Social Change.* Broadleaf Books, 2023, p. 12.

9. Thompson, Derek. "The Case for Vacation: Why Science Says Breaks Are Good for Productivity." *The Atlantic*, 3 Aug. 2012, www.theatlantic.com/business/archive/2012/08/the-case-for-vacation-why-science-says-breaks-are-good-for-productivity/260747/. Accessed 30 Aug. 2024.

10. Resnick, Sofia. "Anti-Abortion Researchers Back Riskier Procedures When Pregnancy Is Threatened." *Ohio Capital Journal*, 23 July 2024, www.ohiocapitaljournal.com/2024/07/23/anti-abortion-researchers-back-riskier-procedures/. Accessed 30 Aug. 2024.

11. UNICEF. "Maternal Mortality." *UNICEF Data*, United Nations Children's Fund, 2023, data.unicef.org/topic/maternal-health/maternal-mortality/. Accessed 30 Aug. 2024.

12. Ibid.

13. Ibid.

14. Ibid.

15. Resnick, Sofia. "Anti-Abortion Researchers Back Riskier Procedures When Pregnancy Is Threatened." *Ohio Capital Journal*, 23 July 2024, www.ohiocapitaljournal.com/2024/07/23/anti-abortion-researchers-back-riskier-procedures/. Accessed 30 Aug. 2024.

16. Che Guevara Reader: Writings on Politics & Revolution, edited by David Deutschmann, Ocean Press, 2003, p. 225.

17. Bush, George W. "Remarks by President George W. Bush at the Dedication of the National Museum of African American History and Culture." *The White House*, 24 Sept. 2016, obamawhitehouse.archives.gov/the-press-office/2016/09/24/remarks-president-george-w-bush-dedication-national-museum-african. Accessed 30 Aug. 2024.

18. Chou, Vivian. "How Science and Genetics are Reshaping the Race Debate of the 21st Century." Science in the News, Harvard University, 12 Apr. 2017, sitn.hms.harvard.edu/flash/2017/science-genetics-reshaping-race-debate-21st-century/. Accessed 25 June 2024.

19. Eligon, John. "Who's Black, Who's African American? A Vibrant Debate, Explained." *The New York Times*, 26 June 2020, www.nytimes.com/2020/06/26/us/black-african-american-style-debate.html. Accessed 30 Aug. 2024.

20. Russell, Bertrand. "In Praise of Idleness." *Harper's Magazine*, Oct. 1932, https://harpers.org/archive/1932/10/in-praise-of-idleness/. Accessed 30 Aug. 2024.

21. Thompson, Hunter S. *The Proud Highway: Saga of a Desperate Southern Gentleman, 1955-1967*. Ballantine Books, 1997, p. 256.

22. Hobbs, Nicola Jane. *Fear-Free Food: How to Ditch Dieting and Fall Back in Love with Food*. Bloomsbury Sport, 2021, p. 45.

23. Orr, David W. Earth in Mind: On Education, Environment, and the Human Prospect. Island Press, 1994.

24. Dunlap, Tori. Financial Feminist: Overcome the Patriarchy's Bullsh*t to Master Your Money and Build a Life You Love. HarperCollins, 2022.

25. Burroughs, William S. *The Western Lands*. Viking Penguin, 1987, p. 125.

26. hooks, bell. Yearning: Race, Gender, and Cultural Politics. Routledge, 2014, p. 227.

27. King, Martin Luther, Jr. *Strength to Love*. Harper & Row, 1963, p. 68.

28. McGlone, Francis, and Susannah Walker. "Four Ways Hugs Are Good for Your Health." Greater Good, Greater Good Science Center at UC Berkeley, 22 June 2021, greatergood.berkeley.edu/article/item/four_ways_hugs_are_good_for_your_health. Accessed 25 June 2024.

29. Bok, Welmoet Tideman. Quoted in Edward W. Bok, *The Americanization of Edward Bok: The Autobiography of a Dutch Boy Fifty Years After*, Charles Scribner's Sons, 1920, p. 423.

30. Park, William. "Why the Wrong People Are Blamed for Climate Change." *BBC Future*, 4 May 2022, www.bbc.com/future/article/20220504-why-the-wrong-people-are-blamed-for-climate-change. Accessed 30 Aug. 2024.

31. Confucius. *The Book of Rites (Li Ji)*, translated by James Legge, vol. 2, Clarendon Press, 1885, p. 227.

32. Van Gogh, Vincent. *The Letters of Vincent van Gogh*. Edited by Mark Roskill, Atheneum, 1963, p. 201.

33. Thich Nhat Hanh. *Peace Is Every Step: The Path of Mindfulness in Everyday Life*. Bantam, 1992, p. 98.

Elsie Gilmore is a writer, mixed media artist, hug evangelist, and activist. *How to Find Joy in a Capitalist Hellscape* is her first full-length publication, inspired by her desire to stop letting social media and other corporate-owned media stoke faux outrage and distract us as we strive to solve the bigger problems of our time. She has participated in large-scale climate change actions and thinks human beings deserve saving from themselves, even the ones we think are yucky.

Her website: elsiegilmore.com
Find her on Instagram: @elsie_gilmore_author
Cover design: Yanuary Navarro at yanuary.com
Illustration of the author: Letisia Cruz at lesinfin.com

Find my book recommendations on Bookshop.org

Find me on Amazon

Need to buy another copy? Here you go!

www.ingramcontent.com/pod-product-compliance
Lightning Source LLC
Chambersburg PA
CBHW070616030426
42337CB00020B/3819